NETWORKED COM
AND COMPLIANCE ....

A Concise Guide to the Legal Issues

Stephen Mason, Barrister

By the same author

Electronic Signatures in Law (LexisNexis Butterworths, 2003)

Chapters

"E-Signature & E-Security: Establishing intent in the electronic environment" for *E-Security Law & Strategy: Practical guide to managing legal risks in information security* edited by Zaid Hamzah (LexisNexis Malaysia and Singapore Edition, 2005)

"Electronic commerce" and "Managing risk on the Internet" (the second chapter with Charles Christian and Rupert Kendrick) for *Internet Marketing Strategies for Law Firms* edited by Nicola Webb (Law Society Publishing, 2003)

E-books

The Year 2000: A guide to the legal issues for business (July 1999)

The Millennium Bug: A guide to the legal issues for business (January 1999)

NETWORKED COMMUNICATIONS AND COMPLIANCE WITH THE LAW

A Concise Guide to the Legal Issues

Stephen Mason, Barrister

Fifth Edition

(Originally published as E-mail and the Internet: a concise guide to the legal issues)

xpl publishing

Published by
xpl law
31–33 Stonehills House
Welwyn Garden City
Hertfordshire
AL8 6PU

ISBN 1 85811 356 3

Typeset by Jane Adams

Cover design by Jane Adams
Cover photography by Jon Adams

Printed in Great Britain by Lightning Source

The content of this book

The content of this guide is deliberately general in nature. It does not deal with any area of law in depth. If the reader needs further information, there are more appropriate sources to acquire a more detailed understanding of any particular area of law. Also, some readers will not need to be reminded of the legal issues within their own expertise.

Many of the examples given in this guide set out the facts in detail. This is to provide the reader with a clear understanding about the nature of the case in order to more fully understand the reason for the decision made.

The content covers the law of England and Wales and is up-to-date at January 2005, but the reader should be aware that changes in the law occur frequently. The contents cannot be taken to be the correct legal view on any matter in depth, and are not a substitute for appropriate professional advice.

Finally, a word of warning: this text only deals with the use of networked communications as between the employer and the employee. It does not deal with matters such as the sending of e-mail communications as a form of marketing.

Acknowledgments

There are a large number of people in the computer industry that have been very patient in answering my questions in relation to all forms of networked communications. You know how you are. Thank you.

CONTENTS

TABLE OF CASES

PREFACE

I have given a great many seminars in relation to the use and abuse of networked communications over the past four years, in particular e-mail, internet use and instant messaging. It is clear that those attending the seminars take a great interest in the issues that arise with the use of networked communications. Although some members of the audience include people responsible for data protection, human resources and, very occasionally, a company secretary, most of those attending are made up of professionals in the IT field. This is disappointing, because the use of networked communications covers all of these disciplines. It is only when organizations recognise the breadth of the matters relating to using networked communications that the problems can be properly recognised and dealt with within an organization.

Compliance – the current buzz word

The reader may be rather fed up with the way the word 'compliance' is bandied about by vendors and members of the media. To a certain extent, I share this feeling. There is no question the use of the word is relevant, but everybody should be asking themselves two highly pertinent questions in relation to compliance:

- What are you complying with?

- What is the purpose of complying with whatever you are complying with?

If you can answer these questions, you are on your way to getting to grips with how to resolve some of the problems you may be facing with networked communications.

No easy legal answer

People constantly question the inability of lawyers to offer a solution that can be applied to all organizations. It is impossible to offer such general guidelines. Some have problems with storage and back up; others have so many subject access requests under the terms of the *Data Protection Act 1998* that they employ several permanent members of staff, whilst others do not know what such a request looks like. Yet other organizations have offices in several jurisdictions, and need to consider not only how to develop and implement the network communications use policy, but how to apply the various data protection laws that apply to different jurisdictions.

The reality

Networked communications covers a wide range of hardware and software. The following list is merely indicative, and even if one or more of the items in the list below is not specifically mention in the text of this book, the reader is requested to accept that what might apply to one form of communication system, will undoubtedly apply all of the items on this list:

- facsimile transmissions

- voice over internet protocol (VoIP)

- e-mail

- use of the internet

- P2P

- instant messaging

- MP3 files

- employee blogs

- computers

- laptop computers

- newsgroups

- chat networks

- mobile telephones

- personal digital assistants

- Blackberry, iPAQ

- content management systems.

Attitudes of employees

The attitudes of employees should make employers sit up and face the issues that accompany the use of networked communications. In its 2004 survey, Web@Work (http://www.websense.com/Web@Work /2004/) illustrated some of the attitudes of employees, the most striking of which were:

- Consistent with previous studies, 51 percent of employees said they spend between 1 and 5 hours per week surfing the internet at work for personal reasons, and those that admitted to personal surfing, spend an average of 2 hours per week doing so.

- The most popular types of non-work related web sites that employees obtain access to at work are news, travel, personal e-mail, and shopping sites.

- Men surf at work more than women. They are twice as likely than women to visit chat rooms or message boards and mp3 sites, and three times more likely than women to visit sports sites. Men are also more apt to visit news, online banking, investment, auction, streaming media, and pornography sites than are women.

- Seventeen percent of employees said they use instant messaging at work, and of those who use instant messaging, 37 percent have either sent or received file attachments via instant messaging while at work. Almost two-thirds (64 percent) of companies do not sanction the use of instant messaging.

- Surfing the web has become as important as drinking coffee. When asked if they would rather give up their morning coffee or their ability to use the internet at work for personal reasons, employees were split: 49 per cent said they would rather give up their morning coffee, while 46 per cent said they would give up access to the internet. More men than women, more non-supervisors than supervisors, and more employees with dial-up rather than broadband at home, are attached to their internet access at work.

Suffice to say that IT managers disagreed with some of these figures: partly because they know that the admissions made by employees in the survey are on the low side. Two very interesting comments made in the printed media of recent highlights the problems faced by employers:

- With respect to downloading copyright materials illegally, the comments of a 28 year old professional by the name of Amir illustrate part of the problem. Ben Hunt in an article 'It's difficult to turn down the offer of free music' in the *Financial Times* Friday October 8, 2004 page 4, reported that Amir admitted the copying of music was illegal and unethical, yet he regards it as an extension of his childhood activities and is quoted as saying 'This is really just an extension of that, and I pretty much decided I was OK with that 15 years ago'. With schools teaching children how to download copyright material from the internet every day (at the behest of the politicians), it is no wonder employers have a difficult job in re-educating younger employees.

- A further example is that of Tim Wanstall, a keyboard player from Athlete, who trained as an actuary, and who took part in an item about becoming self employed in *Metro*, January 10, 2005 page 21. In answer to the question 'What do you miss most about working in an office?' he responded 'Free mineral water. Oh, and sorting your e-mail and browsing the Internet on someone else's time.' Whilst it must be emphasised that this item tends towards the light-hearted, nevertheless his response does help to reinforce, to a certain extent, the findings of the Web@Work survey.

Unions

Some leaders of unions are very familiar with the issues discussed in this text, and work with employers to help resolve the practical problems, especially the complexity over the private use and abuse of the communications system. It is not in the interests of union leaders to put the livelihood of their members at risk by taking an unrealistic stand against monitoring of communications in the workplace. However, I have come across local union officials that make the most bizarre of statements, the most common of which are;

- The *Data Protection Act 1998* does not affect unions.

- Their members have an absolute right to use the organization's communications facilities for personal use.

Both these assumptions are totally incorrect. It will be interesting to know how many unions at national and local level have informed the Information Commissioner that they handle personal data – which they must do, by definition of their purpose in life, at all levels. Second, before they were provided with facilities such as e-mail, it will be interesting to know how many union leaders insisted on maintaining that their members had the right to type up personal correspondence on typewriters provided by their employer during working time, and to post such personal correspondence at the cost of the employer. Clearly the ground rules have changed with the passing of the *Regulation of Investigatory Powers Act 2000*, but even with the provisions contained in the European Convention on Human Rights, no such 'rights' ever existed absolutely.

New forms of communication – new dangers

To seasoned watchers, the rise of instant messaging and blogging is not new. However, some people reading this for the first time might not be aware of instant messaging nor the new form of communicating opinion, called blogging. Instances of employees using these methods of communicating have begun to affect the way employers consider their infrastructure, and an employee has already been dismissed for making unwarranted comments about his employer (details of this case are illustrated in the discussion on defamation).

Similarly, the use of instant messaging has identical problems to the way e-mail is used. Instant messaging is not dealt with in any detail in this text, partly because the legal ramifications of using instant messaging are identical to the use and mis-use of e-mail. In early 2004 one instance came to light in Australia, where instant messaging was one of the forms of communication used by employees of the National Australian Bank. Apparently, an A$180bn loss was blamed on four traders (three in Melbourne, one in London). It seems that these traders engaged in unauthorized transactions in foreign exchange options. They intended to recoup earlier losses when the dealers bet that the Australian and New Zealand dollar would rise and peak against the US dollar, but neither did. The fall-out included comments from the ratings agencies (Standard and Poor, Moody), that the event undermined the bank's credibility in risk management systems. This incidence highlighted the problems of the operational risk management policy inherent in a large and complex organization. It also illustrated the damage that instant messaging can bring to a large organization. Interestingly, the Federal Deposit Insurance Corporation in the USA issued 'Guidance on Instant Messaging' on 21 July 2004, illustrating the seriousness with which financial institutions are expected to treat this form of communicating.

The relevance of instant messaging should not go unnoticed. In a study commissioned by the American Management Association and ePolicy Institute in 2004, it transpired that over one in five employers (or 21 per cent) had employee e-mail and instant messages subpoenaed in the course of a lawsuit or regulatory investigation in the United States of America. This is not going to alter, and the submission of such evidence will increase over time. Only recently, the Financial Services Authority fined Jason Smith and Robin Hutchins for insider dealing, and part of the evidence included an exchange of e-mails. Instant messaging was not used in this instance, but no doubt it will be in future cases.

Leadership is required

It is clear to me that so much hot air is being talked about reputation, but little is actually being done by those responsible. Until directors and senior managers participate in the process of being educated into the concerns relating to the use of networked communications within the organization, they will continue to fail to grasp that it is an issue that will not go away, and their failure to deal with the problems may cause their name to appear in future editions of this text for the wrong reason. Networked communications are here to stay, and the sooner organizations take responsibility for implementing suitable precautions in relation to the issues set out in this text, the better it will be for the employers and their employees. Invariably, the IT department is required to justify the purchase of systems by proving a return on investment. Whilst this is a very important factor to take into account when trying to resolve a problem, nevertheless I hope to illustrate in this text that the costs of the risks may be greater than the cost of trying to resolve the problems.

Stephen Mason
stephenmason@stephenmason.co.uk
Langford, Bedfordshire
April 2005

CHAPTER 1
THE LIABILITY

> E-mail is great for efficiency, simplicity and speed. But what are the legal costs?

Corporate liability

When an employer takes on employees, the authority vested in the employer is delegated to the employee in varying degrees, depending on their position within the organization. The employer becomes liable for the activities of its employees whilst they act within the scope of their employment. This is what is meant by vicarious liability. For this reason, it is possible for the employer to be liable whether employees use the communications infrastructure (to send e-mails or instant messages for instance) from the office or from any other location, such as a home computer.

To reduce risk to the organization, the employer should take reasonable care to prevent improper or illegal activities taking place. For instance, an employer may have a defence in sexual and racial discrimination cases if they can prove they took steps that were reasonably practicable to prevent employees from doing any of the acts complained of. This means an employer needs, in respect of sexual and racial discrimination, to have an anti-discrimination policy in place and to ensure the policy is effectively communicated, monitored and implemented. Organizations must also take active steps to reduce the risk to both the organization and individual employees when using the communications network. If the organization fails to discourage e-mail and internet abuse that introduces racially or sexually offensive material, for instance, the employer can be challenged for failing to protect employees from harassment or discrimination at work – and there is no limit to the amount of compensation that can be awarded.

Some of the areas of liability employers are exposed to when using the communications network include (this list is not exhaustive):

- Defamatory remarks;

- Breach of confidentiality;

- Using and abusing copyright material without permission;

- Negligence in sending viruses to other business;

- Sexual or racial harassment.

Even if the liability of an organization is limited for the acts of its employees, it still has to take into account other issues, such as its reputation and adverse news in press and media reports.

The personal liability of directors

The reader will be aware that some of the past directors of Equitable Life are defending themselves in legal proceedings for the failures of the world's oldest life assurance company. Dealing with such allegations is a time consuming and expensive process, and sometimes the director's liability insurance may not be sufficient to cover all the legal expenses that can arise in such circumstances. A director has a duty to the company, and it is possible for individual directors to be found personally liable for failing to undertake duties implied by law. It is also possible that a director's service contract may require them to provide additional obligations that go beyond the duties set out in law.

Directors cannot avoid dealing with misuse of the communications network within the organization.

Exposure of senior officers in the USA

In the United States of America, Frank Quattrone, a senior officer and Head of the Technology Group with Credit Suisse First Boston, was convicted of obstructing an investigation into the allocation of stock offerings in September 2004. He was sentenced to 18 months' imprisonment and fined US$90,300, although at the time this text was in preparation, he intends to appeal the sentence. Part of the evidence that helped to convict him was the content of two e-mails sent on 4 and 5 December 2000. The e-mail dated 4 December 2000 was sent by the Head of Execution to hundreds of members of the Technology Group. Mr Quattrone authorized this e-mail. The text of the message urged the recipients to comply with the bank's document retention policy and destroy documents that were not required to be retained under the terms of the policy. The e-mail ended:

"We strongly suggest that before you leave for the holidays, you should catch up on file cleaning."

Frank Quattrone sent the subsequent e-mail on 5 December. It had the text of the 4 December e-mail attached, and stated:

"[H]aving been a key witness in a securities litigation case in south texas (miniscribe) i strongly advise you to follow these procedures."

The members of the jury in the second trial decided that Frank Quattrone's e-mail did not help his case.

Ramifications for the organization

As the regulatory authorities gather the pace of their activities across the world, so commercial organizations can expect to face increased pressured to take adequate action to prevent illegal behaviour from taking place, or behaviour that undermines the generally accepted norms of society. A number of examples help to demonstrate the significance that regulators are beginning to have on corporate governance.

Marsh, Inc

In 2004, the Attorney General of the state of New York, Eliot Spitzer, took action against March & McLennan Companies, Inc, and Marsh, Inc for a practice known as 'contingent commissions' that did not provide the best deal for a client, and also for ensuring false bids took place when placing insurance contracts to attract higher premiums. A number of senior executives face criminal charges, one of which, Robert Stearns, a senior vice president and employee of Marsh for over 20 years, has already entered a plea of guilty of scheming to defraud. On 11 March 2003, Robert Stearns sent an e-mail to April Greenwood, a Marsh broker, and instructed Greenwood in connection with another account (Note: a 'B' is a back-up quote to ensure business was secured):

> "Can you get me a B from Zurich. Client will be binding with [incumbent] St. Paul at $270,000 all coverages as expiring. $325,000 should work."

Later that day, in another e-mail, Robert Stearns reiterated his request to Greenwood to "have them issue a B on the lead at $325,000 or more." The next day, an underwriter at Zurich provided a $360,000 quote to Marsh.

The effects of such action can be significant:

- In Bermuda, Ace (whose chief executive is Evan Greenberg) is reported to have dismissed two managers and taken action to alter its practices as a direct response to this action.

- The Chairman and Chief Executive of Marsh, Jeff Greenberg, resigned.

- The share price of Marsh has been reduced significantly as a result of this action.

Financial Services Authority

The Financial Services Authority in the United Kingdom has begun to take proceedings within their remit in respect of breaches of regulations. A number of actions have already taken place, including that of Robert Hutchins, who was an Approved Person working as an equity research analyst in the technology sector at Evolution Beeson Gregory, and Jason Smith, a Chartered Accountant, who was the Finance Director and Company Secretary of I Feel Good (IFG) between early 2000 and July 2003. Both men were friends and former colleagues.

In March 2003, IFG and Dennis Publishing Limited (Dennis) began discussions about a possible takeover. On 15 April 2003, IFG announced that it had received an approach. During the time leading up to the eventual takeover in early May, Jason Smith and Robin Hutchins remained in touch with each other by telephone, the exchange of text messages and e-mail. Mr Hutchins bought a number of shares, staggered over a period of three days, and eventually sold them for a profit of £4,924. Part of the evidence that was available to the FSA included an e-mail sent by Jason Smith to Robin Hutchins at about 9:30 am on 28 April 2003 stating that the Dennis bid had been accepted. Mr Hutchings responded by asking, "Is there no other bid? When is the announcement due?" In an e-mail sent by Jason Smith and received by Mr Hutchins at about 9.35am that day, Smith told Hutchings that there were "no other bids about – 8p looks like the final offer. Without going into all the detail, it is James' best option by a long way".

For this breach of insider dealing, the FSA fined Mr Hutchins £18,000, and Mr Smith £15,000.

Beware the content of an e-mail

It is clear that the meaning of what we say can be taken differently, depending on the circumstances in which it is said. The words in an ill-conceived e-mail may not adequately indicate the inflection or sub-text, unless the writer more thoughtfully considers the content. This aspect of e-mail has begun to affect the way people use e-mail when the prospect of legal action looms. When a problem occurs within an organization, it is perfectly acceptable to ensure the organization adheres to correct procedures and processes. That is why organizations employ lawyers and people with personnel skills. This is what happened in the case of *Stephanie Villalba v Merrill Lynch & Co Inc, Merrill Lynch Europe Limited and Merrill Lynch International Bank Limited*. In this instance, Ms Villalba took action against her employer for unlawful direct sex discrimination, unlawful victimisation, unequal pay and unfair dismissal. Once Ms Villalba's superior mangers became aware that difficulties were occurring with their relationship with Ms Villalba, they began to involve the personnel department when corresponding with Ms Villalba, especially by e-mail. In particular, in the opinion of the members of the employment tribunal at paragraph 150 of their decision, e-mails written by Raymundo Yu (Head of International Private Client Group), Ausaf Abbas (Head of Global Private Client), Sean Woodroffe (International HR Director) and Pauline Cahill (Senior HR Officer and subsequently Head of HR for Europe, Middle East and Africa) at the material time:

> '...clearly show that Mr Yu, Mr Abbas, Mr Woodroffe and Ms Cahill suspected that Ms Villalba might bring a complaint of sex discrimination and equal pay in relation to treatment by Mr Abbas and her bonus award.'

The members of the tribunal reached the conclusion, in paragraph 149, that:

> 'In their emails, the HR department appear to be relishing the conflict and seeking to manoeuvre as one would in a game of chess or poker. The term "checkmate" is used in one email. Margaret Lyng of HR [Head of HR for Global Private Client Europe, Middle East and Africa] describes her as "lining her ducks up" with reference to a request for information of her performance rating of AD in 2001 in an email of 9th January 2003.'

The members of the tribunal had the evidence of the e-mails before them when they assessed the evidence given to them by Mr Woodroffe, Ms Cahill and Mr Yu on this matter. The members of the tribunal in paragraph 150 commented upon the difference between the evidence in the e-mail traffic, and what they said in evidence:

> 'We did not accept either Mr Woodroffe, Ms Cahill or Mr Yu's explanation that whilst they thought she was preparing to bring a legal case, they did not consider what type of case she might bring. None of these witnesses gave this part of their evidence convincingly.'

In particular, the members of the tribunal commented on the actions of Mr Woodroffe, in that '... he did not wish to discuss Ms Villalba's situation by email ... We infer that the reason for his coyness was to avoid a paper trail that could be used in legal proceedings such as this.' By 17 January 2003, the e-mails sent by Mr Abbas to Ms Villalba were either drafted or vetted by the personnel department. By the end of March 2003, Ms Villalba put the matter into the hands of her solicitors. In partial response to this news, Mr Woodroffe sent and e-mail on 29 March 2003 to Mr Abbas, stating 'The fun begins'. The members of the tribunal described this e-mail as 'extraordinary'.

When summing up their findings, the members of the tribunal had the following to say in respect to the content of the later e-mail traffic:

> '254. There was a snide edge and a sneering tone to the emails about Ms Villalba that emerges from mid-January onwards that is not present in earlier emails. It is particularly disappointing to see some of these emanating from a human resources department. We attribute the change to the allegation of discrimination raised by Ms Villalba. We can also see a contrast between the comparatively gentle, somewhat wry, observation of Ms Villalba as "high maintenance" to Ms Matsuoka [General Counsel for International Private Client Group] in early November with the tone of the emails about her from mid-January onwards which further bolsters our conclusion that a significant factor in the denigration and attack, as demonstrated in the emails is on grounds of victimization. We also note that the later emails were written in the consciousness that they might become discoverable in legal proceedings and there is a degree of self censorship by the references to not preferring not to "script on email", but to discuss her over the telephone. It is therefore reasonable for us to infer that the email exchanges were more restrained than the telephone conversations between them around this time.'

There are some lessons to learn from this case:

- E-mail is just another form of evidence that is regularly adduced in all forms of litigation.

- It is only right that an organization uses the resources at its disposal to resolve issues between employees. It is the function of employees in the personnel and legal departments to provide appropriate advice to their employer. In this respect, it is perfectly correct for such employees to advise managers about how to deal with any problems that may occur.

- The advice offered by professionals within the organization, and any e-mail correspondence initiated by such people, will be taken into account by an adjudicator, especially if the e-mail correspondence illustrates the complaint is valid or demonstrates the attitude prevailing within the organization at the time of the complaint.

The content of an e-mail can haunt you

Jack Grubman, a former high-profile telecommunications analyst working for Salomon Smith Barney in the USA, is now aware of this. He sent e-mails in November 1999 that claimed he changed his mind about investing in AT&T, upgrading his opinion to "buy". It was reported that the e-mails were sent in response to a request by Sandy Weill, chairman and chief executive of Citigroup, the world's largest financial services organization to "take a fresh look at AT&T".

The New York state attorney general uncovered the e-mails in November 2002, and Jack Grubman resorted to offering an explanation for his change of mind by suggesting that he "invented a story in an effort to inflate my professional importance". It is reported that he agreed to pay a US$15m fine to settle charges brought by the New York state attorney general, and to be barred from the securities industry for life.

It should also be borne in mind that very senior people may be called upon to leave their jobs, no matter how good they are, if it is demonstrated that they have offended the relevant policy. A recent example is that of Mr Harry Stonecipher, the CEO of Boeing in the

USA. The facts seem to be that Mr Stonecipher had an affair with Debra Peabody, a vice-president of Boeing.

The affair came to light when an anonymous employee intercepted correspondence between the two. The correspondence was described as of being romantic in nature. The employee sent the correspondence to Mr Lewis Platt, the chairman of Boeing. It appears that the correspondence was in the form of e-mail communications.

Mr Stonecipher failed to follow the code of conduct, in that employees are not to engage in any conduct or activity that might raise questions as to the honesty, impartiality, or integrity of the company. Apparently, Mr Stonecipher insisted that all employees follow this code. He was dismissed on 7 March 2005. Leaving aside the important issue of how the employee came to be in possession of the correspondence, this example demonstrates that even the most powerful can be made to leave their job because of inappropriate communications.

People always look for motives

The reader will be aware that Arthur Andersen was convicted (and fined US$500,000) of criminal charges in the United States of America during June 2002 for destroying documents in the knowledge that an investigation had been initiated against Enron. This prosecution demonstrated that one part of one sentence in one e-mail was considered sufficient to seal the fate of the fifth largest accountancy firm in the world. In June 2004, an appeal against this conviction was rejected.

The e-mail that helped the jury reach a guilty verdict

For the members of the jury, the relevant people were David Duncan of Andersen, who handled the Enron audit, and Nancy Temple, one of Andersen's in-house lawyers. David Duncan had a telephone conversation with an employee of Enron about a press release, during the course of which he:

- Warned Enron against describing a set of charges that ran into billions of dollars as "non-recurring". In his opinion, this would not be correct, because such wording might not comply with accounting rules.

- Informed Enron that press releases were a matter for Enron, not Andersen.

- Said Andersen would not let the phrase "non-recurring" be used where Andersen filed documents for which they were responsible.

- Suggested it would be in Enron's interest if different language was used (his advice was ignored).

Mr Duncan recorded his recollection of the conversation in a memorandum sent by e-mail on the 16 October 2001 at 5 pm, and asked Nancy Temple to check his draft. Nancy Temple consulted outside lawyers on this issue. She replied to Mr Duncan's e-mail at 8.39 pm. In her reply, the first two comments were of relevance:

"Dave – Here are a few suggested comments for consideration.

I recommend deleting reference to consultation with the legal group and deleting my name on the memo. References to the legal group consultation arguably is a waiver of attorney-client privileged advice and if my name is mentioned it increases the chances that I might be a witness, which I prefer to avoid

I suggest deleting some language that might suggest we have concluded the release is misleading."

The members of the jury decided this comment in the e-mail sent by Nancy Temple indicated something was not right. They thought there must have been some reason for these comments, and this is why they found Andersen guilty.

The scary bit

Every organization should make a note of the following points:

- Regardless of Nancy Temple's comments, Mr Duncan's memorandum, which was not shredded, made Andersen's position perfectly clear with respect to the contents of the press release.

- The press release issued by Enron made it plain that the figures quoted were not audited. This meant Andersen was not responsible for the accuracy of the figures.

- Although the prosecution did not place much weight on this memorandum, the members of the jury decided to use a single sentence from this document to convict Andersen. This request by Nancy Temple caused the members of the jury to think that there was something wrong, which meant the shredding of documents was also highly suspect.

The lesson

All organizations use e-mail extensively, and instant messaging is also beginning to increase in volumes. At present, many people treat e-mail and instant messaging as an informal extension of an oral conversation. The author is aware of a number of organizations that treat all e-mails as a wholly transient medium. These organizations are wrong to take such a view, especially because some e-mails may be required to be retained by the sender or recipient, as demonstrated elsewhere in this book. Even if e-mails are deleted, they can be recovered. If they are no longer available in the electronic archive, the recipient will probably have a copy. Each e-mail leaves a trail, and it is rare for an e-mail to completely disappear.

Many e-mails tend to lack formality of structure, often do not include the details of the organization required by law and are written using informal language. In combination, these factors can help to convince an adjudicator (whether members of a jury or a judge sitting on their own), that such documents carry *more* weight than documents that are written with further thought. The perception of informality means people tend to record their first thoughts in an e-mail – thoughts that we all know will change as we think about an issue and discuss it with others.

The implication is clear

Organizations must, as a matter of course, ensure all members of staff are made aware of the dangers when using e-mail in particular to communicate, whether internally or externally.

Tips

- For an e-mail that you consider important, check it for spelling first.

- Do not send it immediately, but wait for half a day or overnight before re-reading it.

- If you are happy with the content, send it.

- If not, tinker with the text until it more accurately reflects the message you wish to convey.

- If in doubt, delete it.

CHAPTER 2
TYPES OF MISUSE

> Failing to control the use of networked communications can be an expensive option

E-mail

It may be that the organization permits employees to send and receive personal e-mails. It is debatable whether an organization will be liable for the private communications between employees and friends, although it is possible to argue the employer is liable, because it controls the official stationery, and employees are not permitted to write personal letters on official stationery. Whether an e-mail is considered to be official correspondence will be determined by the content of the e-mail. As a result, a person can send any number e-mails, each of which will fall into a different category. For instance:

- An e-mail discussing official business between employees internally is an internal memorandum.

- A similar e-mail sent out to a third party relating to official business is an external communication, and should be treated as official stationery, by being sent with the same corporate information that is contained on the stationery.

- An extension of a telephone conversation, confirming something, for instance, is a note to be added to a file, whether it is sent to people within the organization or to external addressees, or a mix of internal and external addressees.

- A note to a friend to say you enjoyed the party last night is an item of private correspondence using the organization's resources. The use of e-mail for this purpose may or may not be authorized by the organization.

In many instances the employee has access to the internet, the e-mail system and perhaps instant messaging facilities on their computer, all of which may be supplied to them by the organization. As a result, it can be said that where an employee is permitted to use e-mail for personal use, the employer is also publishing or permitting the comments to be published, because the communication is travelling over lines of communication controlled by the organization.

Whether employees are allowed to use e-mail for personal use or not, it is wise to consider including appropriate clauses in the relevant policy relating to its use, and link failure to comply with the appropriate disciplinary procedures. Where it is decided that employees are not permitted to use e-mail facilities for personal use, it is important to consider the risks associated with permitting employees to use alternative ways of obtaining access to e-mail facilities that cannot be controlled by the organization, such as hotmail and instant messaging.

> **Tips**
>
> - If you decide to permit employees to use e-mail for personal use, consider having separate templates, one for company use and one for personal use.
>
> - Alternatively, contemplate providing separate facilities, such as a stand-alone computer, although this option may still leave the organization open to a legal challenge.

Examples of misuse

E-mails containing inappropriate sexual material

There is always a fine dividing line between encouraging a high level of camaraderie between employees, the quality of which can be beneficial to every organization, and instances where individuals overstep the parameters of what is judged to be acceptable behaviour. Employees should be aware of these boundaries, and their conduct within the scope of their employment must reflect this awareness, especially where they hold a senior position within the organization, as demonstrated by Mike Soden, the Chief Executive of the Bank of Ireland and a director of the Post Office. In May 2004, he resigned from his posts after a regular internal audit of e-mail traffic showed that he broke the terms of the policy relating to the use of the internet. It was reported that he might have accidentally visited a web site selling pornographic images as he was browsing through a series of escort agencies in Las Vagas before visiting the United States.

Where an employee fails to observe this requirement, the organization must take action, as the following examples illustrate.

Mr J F Crook v Manpower plc

Reference for this case: Bury St Edmunds employment tribunal (30 May 2001, Case No 1501774/2000)

Facts

Mr Crook was employed in a senior post as a regional manager with Manpower plc. On 26 June 2000 Mr Crook sent an e-mail to his line manager, Ms Brunton in Edinburgh, requesting authorisation for a salary increase for a female member of staff on the ground that she had worked well and had demonstrated her worth. Ms Brunton replied immediately, providing the authority, and asking "however, out of interest what has she done to demonstrate her worth and how was it measured?" Mr Crook took the comments made by Ms Brunton in her reply as an invitation that carried some sexual innuendo. He answered her e-mail the following day, by giving brief particulars of what the employee had achieved and concluded the e-mail with the words "She was a grrrrrreat shag as well."

A disciplinary meeting was subsequently held on 5 July 2000, and Mr Crook was summarily dismissed for sending an inappropriate e-mail about a subordinate to his line manager, the content of which comprised sexual discrimination, use of offensive language about the subordinate and constituted a serious misuse of the company e-mail system.

Mr Crook argued that the words he used amounted to a private joke to a colleague with whom he had always been on good terms. He thought Ms Brunton would be expecting such a reply. Whilst Ms Brunton accepted that she had, on a few semi-social, work related occasions, engaged in mild horseplay with both male and female colleagues, the members of the tribunal did not consider the reply she made to the first e-mail sent by Mr Crook constituted the innuendo which he attributed to it.

Decision

The members of the tribunal were satisfied that Ms Brunton was justified in treating Mr Crook's reply as amounting to gross misconduct. Given the relative seniority of Mr Crook's position and his management responsibilities, they concluded that Mr Crook was not unfairly dismissed.

Further examples that have not got as far as an employment tribunal include the following:

Norton Rose, solicitors

In December 2000, Claire Swire, the girlfriend of assistant solicitor Bradley Chait in the law firm Norton Rose sent him, amongst other recipients, an e-mail containing a joke. The pair then exchanged a number of e-mails, which referred to a sex act she performed upon him. He sent a copy of the final e-mail to 12 colleagues, who in turn passed it on until millions read it. In this instance, the firm did not dismiss the employees concerned.

Carlyle Group

In May 2001, Peter Chung sent an e-mail to his friends about his move to Korea. He informed recipients about the size of his three-bedroom apartment and how he intended to use each bedroom. He made explicit his intentions towards members of the opposite sex in Korea. Copies of this e-mail were invariably forwarded across the world, and he subsequently resigned from his post with the Carlyle Group.

Credit Lyonnais

In October 2002, Trevor Luxton was suspended from his job as a clerk with Credit Lyonnais after he sent an e-mail to five friends. In this e-mail, Mr Luxton claimed his friend's ex-girlfriend Laura performed a sexual act upon him, during the course of which he simultaneously watched a game of football on the television, drank beer and engaged in a conversation with his girlfriend over the telephone. This e-mail was also sent across the world very quickly.

Hobsons plc

In March 2004, Sharon Dyson, a manager at the student careers advice specialists Hobsons plc, was working in Australia when she sent an e-mail to her boyfriend, Alex Hewson. In the e-mail, Ms Dyson complained that she had to "... write sucky 'thank you' email to clients now, w*nk, w*nk," on behalf of her employer. After this comment, she continued to discuss certain sexual exploits that each performed on themselves when they spoke to each other over the telephone. Apparently Ms Dyson only intended to send the reply to her boyfriend, but she clicked the "Reply to all" icon, and it went to the 30 individuals that her boyfriend sent his original e-mail to. The recipients rapidly disseminated Mr Dyson's e-mail around the world, and it appeared in the national press soon thereafter.

It should be noted that the e-mail sent by Claire Swire was mentioned in most of the reports in relation to the Hobson example, emphasising the fact that the name of Norton Rose continues to be associated with such e-mails, years after the event. All organizations have reputations to uphold – these examples illustrate the need to have appropriate systems in place to protect reputation and reduce risk.

Inappropriate content

When writing the text of an e-mail, it is important to ensure the content is appropriate for the purpose, as the lawyer working for Charles Russell will probably accept, as noted below.

Charles Russell, solicitors

In February 2002, Rachel Walker, a black secretary, took action against the law firm Charles Russell. After Ms Walker handed her notice in, Adam Dowdney, a lawyer in the firm, sent an e-mail to Clive Hopewell, a partner "Can we go for a real fit busty blonde this time? She can't be any more trouble and at least it would provide some entertainment! Mr Hopewell replied, "I was about to say the same!" Ms Walker inadvertently saw the e-mail and complained to the head of personnel, and initiated a claim for sexual discrimination. Although it was reported that the firm would defend the claim, a settlement was reached for what is reported to have been a substantial amount. Both lawyers wrote a letter of apology to Ms Walker.

In addition, it is also important to ensure this attitude is reinforced in the language used in internal documents, as noted in the next example.

Dear Rich Bastard

A short programme entitled "Emails you wish you hadnt sent" broadcast on BBC television during February 2003 illustrated a number of mistakes in relation to the use of e-mail that could have been avoided. According to Tony Hallett, an Analysis Editor at silicon.com, a city bank had cause to apologise to one wealthy client when a form was sent to them, beginning "Dear Rich Bastard". Apparently the form was a standard template, but was sent out as originally devised. The person sending the form out forgot to alter the salutation.

The internet

Where employees are permitted to use the internet, it is crucial to ensure the organization has an appropriate policy in place to deal with any problems relating to misuse that might occur. Below are a number of examples that illustrate the problems that have come about.

Avoid the development of a hostile working environment

It is possible that the office environment may not be comfortable for women in certain circumstances. As a result, an employer could face a claim for sexual harassment, as in the case below.

Ms M Morse v Future Reality Limited

Reference for this case: London (North) employment tribunal (22 October 1996, Case No 54571/95)

Facts

Ms Morse was employed as the Head of Multi-Media at Future Reality Limited from 21 March 1995 to 4 August 1995. She was the only woman to share an office with several men. The men in the office spent a considerable amount of time looking at sexually explicit or obscene images downloaded from the internet, and some of the pictures were drawn to her attention. During this time, a visitor brought in a toy gorilla which, when squeezed, performed a lewd trick.

Whilst it was accepted that these activities were not directed at Ms Morse personally, the men were not seeking to intimidate her and no sexual advances were made to her, she felt uncomfortable working in this atmosphere. She resigned and complained, amongst other things, of sex discrimination on the grounds of harassment. This was based on the pictures, the use of bad language and the general atmosphere of obscenity in the office.

Decision

The members of the tribunal were satisfied that the nature of the pictures and general language and behaviour in the office had a detrimental effect on Ms Morse and she had, as a result, been subject to sexual harassment. Future Reality was held liable because no one in the company had taken any action to prevent the discrimination from taking place. Ms Morse was awarded £11, 940.26 for breach of contract and sexual harassment, £9,793.65 loss of earnings for three months, £750 for injury to feelings and £1,157.65 interest.

Downloading pornographic images

It is surprising how many employees use the internet to download images that indicate their inability to comprehend the damage that may be caused to their employer's reputation.

How many employees have pornographic magazines sent through the post to themselves at work?

For instance, employees do not have pornographic magazines sent to themselves at work, yet some persist in downloading pornographic images over the internet, as the following case illustrates.

Mr P Thomas v London Borough of Hillingdon

Reference for this case: Watford employment tribunal (16, 17 August; 3 December 2001, Case No 3301428/00); EAT/1317/01/MAA

Facts

Mr Thomas was a lead personnel officer who had completed 14 years' service with the London Borough of Hillingdon before he was dismissed on 27 July 2000. He worked in an open plan office, although his desk was in a secluded position and the screen on his computer was not readily visible beyond his desk. In May 2000, the Council gave an increased number of employees the right to obtain access to the internet, including Mr Thomas.

The Borough did not have a code or policy relating to the use of the internet, and did not provide any training or guidance to employees. However, the disciplinary code was incorporated into the employment contract, and instant dismissal was an option where gross misconduct had been established, and the presence of the employee could no longer be tolerated. Mr Thomas was also subject to the Borough's Code of Conduct, which is based on the National Code of Local Government

Conduct. One of the requirements of this Code is: "Employees must conduct themselves at all times to the highest standard of integrity and probity so that there can be no suspicion that they might be influenced by improper motives."

On 13 June 2000, it was discovered that Mr Thomas used his computer to obtain access to the internet to look at web sites showing content of an adult nature. The subsequent investigation indicated that Mr Thomas obtained access to a number of web sites, on the dates, times and for the duration set out below:

23 May 2000	7.08	1.36 minutes
30 May 2000	7.10	8.18 minutes
8 June 2000	8.57	23.59 minutes
9 June 2000	9.03	51.21 minutes

Mr Thomas was suspended on 14 June. During the course of subsequent meetings, Mr Thomas:

- Apologised for his conduct, understood his actions were wrong and said he would not do it again.

- Indicated he went to a web site for an actress, Selma Hayek, from which he had been automatically transferred to web sites containing adult material and discovered he could not extricate himself from these web sites. However, during a disciplinary hearing that took place on 27 July, it was demonstrated to Mr Thomas that he could not have been automatically transferred to web sites containing adult material, because the IT department "swept" such sites regularly to have the automated links removed.

- He admitted entering some web sites intentionally, and also printed five or six images to view the print quality. When asked why he persisted in viewing certain material on four separate occasions, each for a longer period than before, Mr Thomas accepted he deliberately obtained access to the web sites and acted mindlessly.

- He accepted his professionalism and common sense should have prevented him from visiting the web sites. However, he also said he would not have viewed the web sites if there had been a policy in place, because he said that he always followed instructions.

As a result of the investigation, Mr Roger Hackett, Head of Personnel Services concluded:

- Mr Thomas obtained access to web sites that were inappropriate.

- Viewing such web sites amounted to unauthorized use of Council resources.

- There was a danger that others might have seen the material.

- The actions carried out by Mr Thomas were in breach of the Code of Conduct.

- The Borough could no longer place trust in Mr Thomas to deal objectively and professionally with sensitive matters, such as advising on disciplinary matters or people in vulnerable situations.

Mr Hackett decided that Mr Thomas was guilty of gross misconduct. After considering the items offered in mitigation, such as the candid nature of his admissions, his good record, contrition and inexperience of the internet, Mr Hackett concluded that his behaviour had caused fundamental damage to the relationship of trust and confidence between employee and employer. Mr Thomas was summarily dismissed.

Decision

The members of the tribunal decided that the decision to dismiss was outside the range of reasonable responses that a reasonable employer might have adopted in the circumstances. It was found that Mr Thomas had been guilty of misconduct, but not gross misconduct, and therefore the dismissal was unfair. However, it was felt that Mr Thomas made a considerable contribution to his own dismissal, and it was decided that it was just and equitable to reduce his award by 30 per cent.

Having obtained employment as a Personnel Officer with CPM International in October 2000, his revised award amounted to a total of £13,775.79, comprising: Basic Award £2,254; Compensatory Award £6,845.33 and loss of Statutory Rights £4,676.46. He was also granted a further £1,629.21 for wrongful dismissal (this figure included loss of pension contributions).

Appeal

The London Borough of Hillingdon appealed against the decision of the tribunal to an Employment Appeal Tribunal. The members of the Appeal Tribunal held that it was wrong for the members of the tribunal to substitute their own, more lenient view of the employee's activities. It was a reasonable response for an employer to dismiss an employee for obtaining access to pornography during working hours.

Misuse of internet facilities can affect your reputation

Individuals as well as the organizations they work for or represent can suffer where their actions are brought to light, although some individuals are fortunate enough not to have their names revealed, as in the next example.

Richmond Council

In April 2001 a councillor from Richmond-upon-Thames Council was caught surfing for pornography using a laptop computer owned by the council. An internal investigation was set up by the borough's standards panel after a random check of staff laptop computers found the councillor had logged in to pornography web sites. The councillor was reprimanded for misusing council property. He was not identified.

Failure to put sufficient controls in place to prevent problems from occurring are, perhaps, a major source of embarrassment, as noted by the following example:

Safeways supermarket

In the short programme entitled "Emails you wish you hadnt sent" broadcast on BBC television during February 2003, Brid Fitzpatrick told viewers that she was on the Safeways shopping list. She would look through e-mails sent to her about various offers, and decide whether to buy groceries or not. On one occasion, she received an e-mail with a number of crude nursery rhymes set out in the body of the e-mail. A member of staff sent this e-mail. Apparently, the member of staff accidentally typed in Brid Fitzpatrick's unique number (apparently Safeways do not identify people by reference to personal e-mail addresses, but by numbers). Safeways subsequently apologised and offered a case of wine in recompense.

Where employees misuse the communications system

Employees should be aware that their improper behaviour can lead to disciplinary proceedings being taken against them. Where an employee initiates activities that are not appropriate within the working environment, dismissal can be an appropriate response, as demonstrated by the following case.

Mr R A Pennington & Mr D Beverly v Holset Engineering Limited

Reference for this case: Leeds employment tribunal (30 August and 7 November 2000, Case No 1802184/00 and 1802185/00)

Facts

Mr Beverly was employed by Holset Engineering as an Information Technology Manager from 11 August 1980 to 16 March 2000, and Mr Pennington was employed as the Groups Inwards Inspector from 10 August 1981 to 13 March 2000. In February 2000, Mrs Bateson, the Human Resources Leader, was informed by an employee (with responsibilities for human resources) about e-mails that were circulating within the corporate e-mail structure. The nature of the e-mails was described as offensive. In addition, the distribution of such e-mails constituted a misuse of the system, which was intended for business use.

Mr Beverley sent the e-mail that triggered an investigation into this problem to another employee who found the content to be offensive and unacceptable. It appears that this particular e-mail was probably intended for another employee. Miss Rennie, a Human Resources Manager, was requested to conduct a full investigation. This took her a week, during the course of which she discovered groups of employees who were involved in sending and receiving offensive e-mails. Of all those involved, Mr Beverly and Mr Pennington were the worst offenders.

Both men were dismissed as the result of internal disciplinary proceedings. A number of other employees were also disciplined. Some received a written warning and others received final written warnings, in accordance with the degree of their culpability.

Decision

The members of the tribunal found that the summary dismissal of both employees was within the reasonable response of a reasonable employer.

Where gross misconduct of employee is clear, but the employer waived a breach of contract by the employee

It may be that the organization can demonstrate the conduct warrants dismissal, but care should be taken how the decision is made to dismiss, as the following case illustrates.

Mark Paul Humphries v V H Barnett & Co London

Reference for this case: London South industrial tribunal (July 7, 1998, Case No 2304001/1997)

Facts

Mr Humphries was employed by V H Barnett & Co from 1 June 1996 until 31 July 1997 as the IT manager. He downloaded a total of 103 pictures of sexually explicit material, some of which involved animals, all of which were found on the hard disk. Mr Humphries was subsequently dismissed after a cursory search on the computer he used at work, although the letter from his employers dated 31 July claimed he was put on gardening leave on the grounds of lack of work, and he was requested to be available if required.

The police subsequently found further material. As a result, his employers wrote another letter to him dated 14 August, informing him that he was instantly dismissed from the date of the first letter because he had mis-used the company time and equipment to an extent that was considered to be gross misconduct and a breach of his contract. There was no internet use policy in place, and he was permitted to obtain access to the internet for innocent purposes, such as visiting the web site for the football team he supported, Leeds United Football Club.

Decision

The Chairman (sitting alone) decided that unauthorized use of the internet did not of itself constitute grounds for instant dismissal. He distinguished between surfing the internet for innocent purposes and downloading pornographic images. Although the Chairman reached the conclusion that Mr Humphries was guilty of misconduct sufficient to justify summary dismissal, the employer waived its right to dismiss Mr Humphries by affirming the contract in their letter of 31 July, rather than accepting the breach of contract by Mr Humphries. The contract was terminated on 14 August.

Mr Humphries was awarded damages of £542.13 for wrongful dismissal.

Contravention of established codes of conduct and breaching trust and confidence

Many organizations, both public and commercial, ask employees to refrain from treating the work place as an extension of their outside interests. The organization has a particular purpose to pursue, and has a reputation to uphold. It is possible to dismiss an employee where they breach the trust expected of them, either because of the position they hold or because of the nature of their job.

Mr I Parr v Derwentside District Council

Reference for this case: Newcastle upon Tyne employment tribunal (September 23, 1998, Case No 2501507/98)

Facts

Mr Parr was employed by Derwentside District Council from 23 March 1981 until he was dismissed on 6 January 1998. During the summer of 1997 he obtained access to sexually explicit and pornographic material while at work. When questioned about the images he had downloaded from the internet, Mr Parr accepted he had obtained access to them. He justified his actions by claiming he was concerned how easy it was to obtain access to the material, and expressed his concern that juveniles could see the material. He was subsequently dismissed after a further hearing, in which it was decided that the offence was a serious matter.

Another employee was also dismissed for similar offences, and a third employee resigned before disciplinary action could be taken.

At an appeal hearing, the elected councillors confirmed the decision to dismiss Mr Parr. It was established that the aggravating features of the case had been the nature of the material that was viewed, that the employee was a public servant, that he had misused the council's equipment and time, that he was a senior officer and he had obtained access to the material deliberately. In addition, the employee had broken the officers' code of conduct and damaged the trust and confidence placed in him as a senior manager. In the process, he had brought the council and directorate of community services into disrepute. Mr Parr offered the explanation that he had "got stuck" in the pornographic material and he had viewed it on two further occasions because he was concerned that juveniles could view it. This explanation was not accepted.

Decision

The members of the tribunal accepted that the decision to dismiss the applicant was within the range of responses of a reasonable employer.

Beware web sites that cause you to innocently download obscene images

There are two main ways in which the visitor can unwittingly download files that contain pornographic images or images that are meant for paedophiles. First, a web address can be mistyped, taking the visitor to a web site with pornographic images. One good example is to mistype www.whitehouse.gov. This address may not get the visitor to the web site of the President of the USA. Once on the site, the owners hope the visitor will decide to stay and browse. Even if the visitor does not stay on the web site, the computer may have downloaded images to the cache of the browser. This means the images remain on the computer until they are deleted.

Paedophiles pass their images using a more subtle method. It is possible to download details of a perfectly innocent looking web site. If it contains hidden images, it will probably be a spoof site. In the coding for the page, the images will have been set with a height and width of zero, which makes the images invisible. However, the images are still there and they are downloaded with the rest of the web page on to the computer. The owner may not know the images are there, but they will be in the temporary web page file. Apparently the Wonderland ring of paedophiles used this method to share and distribute the images they sold.

Obtaining access to the internet for personal use

Where an organization provides its employees with access to the internet, the next problem is whether the facility can be used for private benefit, and if so, what amount of time spent using the resource can be construed as reasonable. This is not an easy problem to resolve where employees have unlimited access to the internet without supervision, as the following case illustrates.

Mrs L J Franxhi v Focus Management Consultants Limited

References for this case: Liverpool employment tribunal (29 July 1999, Case No 2102862/98); *The Times*, June 16, 1999

Facts

Mrs Franxhi was the personal assistant to Mr Jones and Mr Michael Staniland, directors of a small firm of management consultants called Focus Management Consultants Limited between 10 June 1996 and 23 July 1999. During the course of Mrs Franxhi's employment she was given several increases in salary and increased responsibilities. In the early part of 1998 Mrs Franxhi informed the company that she was pregnant. As a result, the company had a telephone line installed to her home. This enabled her to work flexible hours in the office or at home.

In the early part of 1998, Mr Jones noticed Mrs Franxhi was sending personal mail and parcels out, using stamps purchased by the company. As a small company, the directors relied on the minimum of regulation and the maximum of trust. It appeared Mrs Franxhi had abused that trust and set a bad example to the rest of the staff. A disciplinary hearing was held on 1 July 1999 in relation to this matter, and Mrs Franxhi was given a final written warning. Less than three weeks later, Mr Jones discovered that Mrs Franxhi had used the internet extensively during working hours over a number of days for the private purpose of booking a holiday. The use was not during the lunch break. When challenged about her use of the internet, Mrs Franxhi stated she only used it once, during her lunch break. A disciplinary hearing was arranged for 23 July 1998. There was no policy in place offering advice with respect to employee's use of the internet. When asked whether she thought her extensive use of the internet was reasonable, she said it was debatable. As a result of this hearing, Mrs Franxhi was dismissed without notice. The employers decided that her use of the internet was only part of the reason for dismissal. The employer was also influenced by her betrayal of trust, that she lied about her use of the internet, and her misuse of the company facilities to obtain access to the internet for a private purpose was close in time to the previous warning.

Mrs Franxhi claimed the company dismissed her because she was pregnant.

Decision

The majority members of the employment tribunal found that Mrs Franxhi was correctly dismissed, although she was awarded a month's pay in lieu of notice. It was felt that she must have known that her wholesale use of the internet was not acceptable to her employer. As a result, her dismissal for misconduct was reasonably justified. The majority members also decided that Mrs Franxhi was not dismissed for being pregnant. Evidence was adduced to show that Mr Jones helped prepare a case for his wife when she was dismissed for being pregnant, and he had very strong feelings about the injustice for a dismissal for that reason.

The minority member did not agree with the majority decision, stating that the employers did not genuinely believe that what Mrs Franxhi did was misconduct, nor was it wrong for her to use stamps and the internet owned by the company for her private use. The minority member also considered Ms Franxhi was dismissed because of her pregnancy.

Commentary

It is pertinent to note the reasons why the majority thought the employer's actions were reasonable:

- The employer genuinely believed Mrs Franxhi abused their internet facility.

- The employer had reasonable grounds for their belief, together with evidence, in the form of the printed records from the computer.

- A reasonable investigation was carried out into the accusations. A disciplinary meeting was convened at which Mrs Franxhi was able to make what representation she wanted.

- Dismissal was a reasonable option for the employers, in that Mrs Franxhi was less than frank in her explanations, she set a poor example to junior staff and the employer had issued a final written warning.

The perspective for employers

From the examples given above, and as discovered by Holset Engineering in the case of *Mr R A Pennington & Mr D Beverly v Holset Engineering Limited*, when employers discover the internet or e-mail facilities have been misused by one or two employees, further investigation reveals many more employees are involved with the distribution of offensive material than is immediately apparent.

> **The process of investigating a complaint can be expensive, which adds to the cost of running any organization.**

In the case of *Pennington & Beverly*, the company e-mail system was investigated for one week. A full analysis of the material was then made before consideration was given to taking disciplinary action. Where an e-mail policy is put into operational effect, such a costly investigation is less likely to be as necessary.

CHAPTER 3
LEGAL LIABILITY OF THE EMPLOYER

> Most organizations cannot afford to ignore the wide range of risks associated with the use of networked communications

The range of risks that an organization is exposed to when permitting employees to use e-mail, the internet, instant messaging, computer to computer (P2P) and similar methods of communication connected to the network, is wide and varied. The issues set out in this chapter illustrate the risks, which in turn demonstrate the need for every organization to provide adequate training to employees. Training should be more than merely sending a copy of the relevant policy to the employee and asking them to acknowledge receipt of the policy. The policy should be written in such a way that it covers the risks to both the employer and employee. This is because where an employee fails to adhere to the policy, they face the possibility of dismissal, and employees should be made fully aware of the risks they face if they fail to abide by the policy.

Defamation

The ramifications are clear for any organization encouraging employees to use e-mail and instant messaging to communicate with people, both internally and externally. If defamatory comments are made, the organization itself could be found partly liable to the party that is subsequently injured. Employers will probably wish to ensure their employees do not defame others during their employment, although the individual that made the defamatory remarks will be primarily liable. However, the claimant is less likely to pursue the originator of the comment if there is an organization with the resources to pay the damages and legal costs of a successful action.

The nature of the internet is such that an e-mail, when sent, will be stored at intermediate points across the infrastructure. Also, multiple copies will exist of the same e-mail, depending on the number of people it is sent to. Taking into account the way e-mail is disseminated, it could be argued that it can only be read if it is intercepted. If this is correct, e-mail will be published only if somebody can read it. For example, if an employee has the responsibility to check e-mails in an organization before they are sent, it is possible that the comments written will be published. However, the person responsible for reading the e-mail might not be able to read every message because of the volume sent each day. In such a situation, proof will probably be required to demonstrate that the e-mail was read, and therefore published.

As for instant messaging, any problems that may occur will probably depend on whether the message has been recorded in some way. Organizations will need to consider whether to record instant messaging in the same way as they do for e-mail. It does not follow that every organization needs to record instant messages. In all probability, a regulator may require the recording of all relevant communications, without specifying the form of communication. In such circumstances, every form of communication will be covered by the guidance.

More recently, some companies have begun to encourage the use of blogs in the workplace, but the same issues that apply to any other form of communication, as outlined in this chapter, will apply to opinions offered by employees on corporate blog sites, especially relating to defamation. The reader should be aware of the first dismissal for keeping a blog in the United Kingdom occurred in January 2005. Joe Gordon, 37, was paid £12,000 a year as a senior bookseller at the Princes Street East End branch of Waterstone's in Edinburgh for 11 years. According to press reports, he was dismissed for bringing the company into disrepute after his blog – *Woolamaloo Gazette* – made satirical remarks about his working life after referring to the company as "Bastardstone's" and one of his managers as "Evil Boss". At the time this text was written, it is reported that he has appealed his dismissal within the organization, and may, if not successful, make an application to an employment tribunal for unfair dismissal.

The liability

Defamation, which can be either slander or libel, has been described as the lowering of someone in the minds of right thinking people. This concept obviously changes as each generation alters it values. Invariably, the arbiters will be members of a jury, because most libel and slander cases are determined in this way in England and Wales.

How you can defame

It is possible that the same comment can be defamatory of one person, but not another. To say a motor racing driver is a mediocre driver might be to defame her. The same comment addressed to Mr Average driver will, probably, be more accurate than the recipient wants to hear, but it will not be defamatory of Mr Average. Another way of defaming an individual is to pass comments without naming the person. Providing enough people are aware of the special information relating to the person referred to, the views that have been expressed can be defamatory.

It is also possible to defame a person unintentionally. Reference to a fictional character might be dangerous where there is a person alive that is identical to the fictional personality. Additionally, you might refer to a person accurately but fail to identify them properly. In such a case, the person you have referred to might be mistaken for somebody else.

A person can be defamed very easily in electronic format, especially when abbreviations and jargon are used widely – it is important to take care to avoid any misunderstanding when sending e-mail.

Libel

A person commits libel when they publish a defamatory statement about an individual to a third person in a permanent form. When a person has successfully demonstrated that they have been defamed in this way, it is assumed that they have suffered general damage. The person defamed does not have to prove they suffered any damage. It is for members of the jury to assess the value of the compensation to be paid. There is a new publication, and therefore a new cause of legal action, each time the defamatory message is read by a different person.

Slander

A person commits slander where they transmit a defamatory statement about a person verbally or in a non-permanent form. Generally, if a person proves they have been defamed in this way, they then must also prove they have suffered damage.

Whether a posting on the internet is libel or slander

The action taken by Dr Laurence Godfrey in 1994, as outlined below, claimed the defamatory statements were either "libel or slander". The case was settled out of court, so a decision has yet to be made by a judge on this issue in England and Wales. This is important, because of the different approach to damages between libel and slander. Whilst no decision has been made whether a defamatory statement made on the internet is libel or slander, it is probable that e-mail will be construed as a permanent publication, and therefore will be libel.

Dr Laurence Godfrey and Philip Hallam-Baker

Facts

Phillip Hallam-Baker is an academic and employee of CERN (the European Laboratory for Particle Physics) that was largely responsible for establishing the internet in Europe. Mr Hallam-Baker posted eight articles on a Usenet group about Dr Laurence Godfrey, a former physicist at the German Electron Synchrotron Laboratory. Dr Godfrey took legal action in 1994 and the case was settled out of court.

The writ alleged the defamatory statement was "libel or slander". The case was settled by agreement between the parties. As a result, it is not certain whether a posting on the internet is libel or slander, although it is probable that it will be treated as libel.

Who can be liable

Anybody who is a party to a libel can be sued, including the author, the publisher, the distributor, the printer (if printed as a book) and any other person involved in the chain. As a result:

- A service provider or the operator of a bulletin board may find themselves liable (although Internet Service Providers do have some defences).

- An employee and their employer can be found liable where the employee sends a defamatory comment during the course of their employment.

- Any person forwarding a defamatory e-mail (including attachments).

The *Defamation Act 1996*, which came into force on 4 September 1996, defines who is liable and what must be proved to establish a successful defence. There are also general defences to defamation, which are justification, fair comment and privilege (which covers confidential information between a professional adviser and their client).

Internal e-mail

Internal e-mails are subject to the law of defamation in the same way as any other form of publication. The following examples serve to indicate how serious the problem can be.

David Eggleton and Asda Supermarket

Facts

David Eggleton, had cause to complain about a joint of meat he purchased from the Asda branch located in Spondon, Derby in 1995. E-mails, with the heading "refund fraud, urgent, urgent urgent", were sent to other stores in the area after he was refunded the cost of the meat. The content of the message gave details of the complaint, together with details of his appearance and car registration number. Mr Eggleton

---

found out about the e-mail when he went to a local Asda branch, at their request, to offer advice about security. Until Mr Eggleton was invited to offer the Asda branch advice on security matters, they were not aware that he was a policeman and a crime prevention officer.

Conclusion

The claim was settled out of court. Asda paid an agreed sum in compensation to PC Eggleton.

Western Provident Association Limited v Norwich Union Healthcare Limited and Norwich Union Life Insurance Company Limited

References for this case: *Financial Times*, 18 July 1997; *The Times*, 18 July 1997

Facts

Employees of Norwich Union spread rumours, distributed internally by e-mail, that Western Provident was being investigated by the Department of Trade and Industry and that the group was close to insolvency. Western Provident obtained an order that required Norwich Union to provide a copy of the relevant e-mail. Western Provident was also granted an order requiring the company secretary of Norwich Union to examine its employees in sales to determine whether anybody had repeated the defamatory remarks to potential customers, and produce an affidavit in which the results were set out in full.

Conclusion

Norwich Union settled out of court by paying Western Provident £450,000, admitted the rumours were false, deeply regretted such e-mails were sent and sincerely apologised to Western Provident for the dissemination of the rumours.

Exoteric Gas Solutions Limited and Andrew Duffield v BG plc

Reference for this case: [1999] LTL 24 September 1999, The Independent, Thursday 24 June 1999

Facts

Mr Duffield was employed by British Gas as a student engineer in 1974. He spent the next 22 years with the company, becoming Manager of District Operations for the Thames Valley West district with responsibility for 400 staff. During Mr Duffield's last three years, British Gas was transformed into a commercial operation. It was split in February 1997 into two separate companies. BG Plc ran the gas distribution network for the UK through its Transco subsidiary. Mr Duffield's immediate superior in his last year was Mr Chris Lefevre, one of four Area Directors and a member of Transco's Top Management Team.

As a result of the changes to the market in gas, Mr Duffield decided, in June 1996, to leave British Gas and form his own company with the intention of competing with Transco in the gas connection market. He informed Mr Lefevre that month. He was only required to give three months' notice, but because of his particular knowledge and experience, he agreed to remain with Transco until the end of the year to make sure that a smooth transition could take place.

Companies working in this area can only compete with Transco with the co-operation of Transco. This is because, in the majority of cases, Transco needs to provide information about the existing gas network and to provide a quotation for its charges to make the final connection to the gas mains. Since the inception of his company, Mr Duffield experienced considerable difficulties in dealing with British Gas. Three months after Mr Duffield's company began trading, Mr Lefevre wrote the following e-mail. It was dated 27 March 1997 and headed "EGS":

"We are dealing with a high level complaint concerning this company (i.e. EGS) and the alleged misuse of Transco information. Could you ensure that you and your staff have no dealings with this company or with its principal (Andrew Duffield) until further notice."

The e-mail was addressed to all of the Managers of District Operations of British Gas and to a number of other senior managers within the company. The e-mail also contained instructions for it to be circulated to all staff, some 10,000 employees of Transco.

The contents of this e-mail alleged there had been strong grounds that Mr Duffield had misused Transco's confidential information, and the alleged misconduct was so serious and the case against him so strong, that Transco employees were prohibited from having any further dealings with Mr Duffield or his company. Neither the allegation that Mr Duffield had misused Transco information, nor the suggestion that British Gas were dealing with a complaint concerning EGS was true.

Conclusion

British Gas paid £101,000 into court, which was accepted. As a result, a trial did not take place. Although British Gas refused to apologise for its actions, it gave an undertaking not to repeat the allegations. The settlement included the money paid into court and an estimated £125,000 in legal fees.

External e-mail

One case has been brought before the courts relating to external e-mails sent by employees that contained defamatory material. The employer, Thames Water, was not involved with the legal action, although the employee's employment contract was terminated. This case illustrates the point that an employer may not be liable every time an employee sends e-mails whilst using the employer's computer.

Takenaka (UK) Limited and Brian Corfe v David Frankl

Reference for this case; LTL 1 November 2000; ILR 11 December 2000 (Alliott J, Queens Bench Division, 11 October 2000); EBCase Volume 100 Number 2/1 May 2001 (Appeal).

Facts

David Frankl was a past employee of Takenaka. He sent three e-mails, purporting to be sent from a person claiming to be Christina Realtor, to his previous boss, Brian Corfe in April, May and June 1999. The e-mails falsely accused Mr Corfe of having an affair for 18 months, fathering a child, refusing to support the child and threatening to kill his mistress. The company was accused of hypocrisy, double standards and callousness. It took months for Takenaka to track down Frankl, an employee of Thames Water working in Turkey at the material time, and to prove that the e-mails were sent from his laptop computer.

Decision

Mr Justice Alliott awarded Takenaka £1,000 by way of general damages and £25,000 in damages to Mr Corfe. In addition, a permanent injunction was granted against Mr Frankl and he was ordered to pay £100,000 in costs. The decision in this case was appealed on 7 March 2001. The members of the Court of Appeal dismissed the appeal.

Obscene publications

The relevant legislation relating to obscene publications is the *Obscene Publications Act 1959* (the *Obscene Publications Act 1964* extended the provisions of the 1959 Act to having an obscene publication for gain). The test for whether an article is obscene is set out in section 1(1):

> "For the purposes of this Act an article shall be deemed to be obscene if its effect or (where the article comprises two or more distinct items) the effect of any one of its items is, taken as a whole, such as to tend to deprave and corrupt persons who are likely, having regard to all the relevant circumstances, to read, see or hear the matter contained or embodied in it."

It must be understood that obscene material does not just mean sexual depravity. It can also refer to drugs or extreme violence. If an obscene publication is held, "having" is defined as having an article in "ownership, possession or control", although simple possession is not a crime except in relation to child pornography.

An "article" is taken, by section 1(2), to mean anything containing matter to be read or looked at, any sound record, any film or picture. "Publication" includes, by section 1(3), distributing, selling, hiring, giving, lending, showing or playing. This section was amended in 1994 to ensure the meaning also covers transmission of data where the article is stored electronically. If a person gives somebody a password that allows them to gain access to an obscene or indecent publication, they are deemed to be publishing for the purposes of committing an offence.

> **The members of the jury decide whether an article is obscene, which means a prosecution does not always succeed.**

The defences to publication of obscene matter are:

- The publication was in the interests of science, literature, art or learning, or of other objects of general concern.

- Not having examined the article, the accused did not have any reasonable cause to believe the article was obscene.

Abusive images of children

Whilst mere possession of adult pornography does not break the law, possession of indecent images of children certainly does. In accordance with the *Criminal Justice Act 1988*, it is an offence to possess an indecent photograph of a child under the age of 16 years. The term "pseudo photographs", which is an image created by a computer, was included as a result of the *Criminal Justice and Public Order Act 1994*.

Under the provisions of section 1 of the *Protection of Children Act 1978*, it is an offence to:

- To take, or permit to be taken, or to make any indecent photograph (photograph includes pseudo-photographs) of a child; or

- Distribute or show such photographs; or

- To have in your possession such photographs with a view to distributing them or showing them to others; or

- Publish or cause to be published any advertisement likely to be understood as conveying that the advertiser distributes or show such indecent photographs.

There are defences to the possession of child pornography:

- The accused can show that they had a legitimate reason to do the act that amounted to the committing of the offence.

- The accused had not seen the photographs and did not know or had no cause to suspect them to be indecent.

- The photographs were sent to the accused without any prior request from them and they did not keep them for an unreasonable length of time.

Clearly, organizations need to ensure members of staff are aware of the risks they face if they download and distribute such materials. Not only could the individual employee face dismissal and subsequent prosecution, but the organization will also face embarrassing and unwanted publicity over the matter, as the following example demonstrates.

> **Atkins v Director of Public Prosecutions; Director of Public Prosecutions v Atkins**
>
> **Reference for this case:** [2000] 1 WLR 1427, QBD
>
> **Facts**
>
> Dr Anthony Rowan Atkins was a university lecturer at the University of Bristol, Department of English, who browsed the internet for indecent photographs of children in October 1997. He did not know that the pictures were cached in the temporary internet file, but he deliberately saved a number of files in the J directory. He was convicted by the metropolitan stipendiary magistrate at the Bristol Magistrates' court on 27 May 1999 of 10 offences of having in his possession indecent photographs of children, nine from the temporary file and one from the J directory. He was fined £50 on each charge and ordered to pay £350 in costs. An order was made that he should register with the police under the *Sex Offenders Act 1997* for five years.
>
> He was acquitted of a further 24 charges, some of which related to the files deliberately saved in the J directory. One reason why the magistrate acquitted Dr Atkins of these charges is because Dr Atkins was charged at a late stage, and the date he was charged was beyond the point laid down for the offences to be effective. The higher court had the power to permit the offences to be heard out of time.
>
> **Appeal**
>
> Dr Atkins appealed against his conviction for possessing indecent photographs of a child because he claimed he held the photographs for genuine academic research. The prosecutor appealed against his being acquitted of the further 24 charges.

Simon Brown LJ and Blofeld J held:

- Where academic research was put forward as a defence, the question was whether the defendant was a genuine researcher with no alternative but to have indecent photographs in his possession. Adjudicators were entitled to be sceptical about whether this defence is made out, and in this case the magistrate was correct to convict.

- Dr Atkins should not have been convicted of possession in respect to the photographs stored in the cache, because he was not aware of the existence of the cache or what it did, and therefore could not be said to have knowingly had possession of these particular photographs.

- The defendant should have been convicted of intentionally placing the photographs in the J directory, because he knew what he was doing. It was ordered that the case be remitted with a direction to convict Dr Atkins of the offences where he deliberately saved photographs in the J directory.

Offences committed by the organization and liability of the officers

Failure to deal adequately or at all in respect of child pornography can lead to prosecution under the provisions of the *Protection of Children Act 1978*. Section 3 provides that a body corporate can be guilty of an offence where it is proved:

> "that the offence (i.e. downloading child pornography) occurred with the consent or connivance of, or was attributable to any neglect on the part of, any director, manager, secretary or other officer of the body, or any person who was purporting to act in any such capacity he, as well as the body corporate, shall be deemed to be guilty of that offence and shall be liable to be proceeded against and punished accordingly."

Being found guilty of this offence can lead, where the offence is dealt with by indictment in the Crown Court, to a maximum period of imprisonment of 10 years or a fine or both. If dealt with by summary proceedings in the Magistrates Court, the maximum term of imprisonment is six months or a fine or both.

Breach of confidential information

The attributes of e-mail, instant messaging and electronic documents in general make it very easy for employees to send trade secrets and other information of a confidential nature to third parties. Whilst it is possible for confidential information to be sent innocently, a significant risk is from disgruntled employees. Even before the organization is aware that an employee will leave their employment, it is probable that a dissatisfied employee will send information out of the company by way of e-mail before they leave. Ideally, all employees will have confidentiality clauses in their employment contracts, although where there is no express contractual obligation of confidentiality, a duty may well arise as between employer and employees in certain circumstances.

> **Employees have been discovered to have operated a business at work using their employers' e-mail system and database.**

The organization may have written contracts in place between themselves and third parties to protect information between legal entities. It is therefore incumbent upon employers to ensure employees are fully aware of the potential for a claim for a breach of confidence if sensitive commercial information is sent, copied or forwarded to unauthorized third parties by an employee without permission.

> **How often do employees send files home without permission?**

The following case illustrates that where an employer fears an employee has broken the contractual duty of confidentiality, action can be taken.

Mr Alan James Winder v The Commissioners of Inland Revenue

Reference for this case: Ashford employment tribunal (20 April 1998, Case No1101770/97/SM)

Facts

Mr Winder was employed by the Inland Revenue as a Valuation Referencer in the Valuation Office at Bromley between 8 June 1987 and 14 July 1997. On 3 September 1996, a letter was left anonymously on the District Valuer's chair at the Bromley Office. Amongst other items, the envelope included a note saying, "This is the contents of Alan Winder's

'OFFICE POWER' docs". It also included a letter, produced on Mr Winder's computer, which was dated 29 August 1996 and addressed to the National Socialist Alliance, offering to disclose names of taxpayers and ratepayers from confidential records held by the Inland Revenue.

The documents were passed to the Human Resources Division (Conduct and Discipline) Section in Nottingham on 9 September 1996 and Mr Winder was later interviewed on 8 May 1997 by the investigating officer and a colleague. He admitted writing the letter and accepted he intended to use the Inland Revenue's computer system to obtain names and addresses of people who infiltrated the National Socialist Alliance, although he had not supplied any information since writing the letter.

Mr Winder was subsequently dismissed on 14 July 1997, because it was considered that there had been a fundamental breakdown of confidence and trust between employer and employee, and that there was a risk that the rules of confidentiality would be broken if he remained in the employment of the Inland Revenue. Mr Winder appealed against this decision, although he did not attend the hearing on 21 October 1997 when his appeal was dismissed.

Decision

The tribunal considered the Inland Revenue was reasonably entitled to take the view that the letter written by Mr Winder amounted to serious misconduct, and dismissal was the appropriate penalty in the circumstances.

Receiving military secrets without trying

In the short programme entitled "Emails you wish you hadnt sent" broadcast on BBC television during February 2003, 16-year-old Claire McDonald told of the six-month period during which she received various e-mails relating to military secrets. Claire said she received about 2,000 e-mails from the Ministry of Defence, HMS Illustrious and the Pentagon. On one occasion, she received the New Zealand Defence Strategy for 2000 – 2001. Eventually, the sheer volume of e-mails caused her computer to collapse. It took Claire some time to make people realise that she was receiving these e-mails. She subsequently spoke to officers in the Pentagon. Apparently, somebody had mis-typed an address on an e-mail, and the mis-typed address was that of Claire. She then became party to large volumes of material.

Confidential information can encompass a wide range of information, including the names and addresses of clients, for instance, as demonstrated in the example below.

Weil, Gotshal & Manges

In April 2002, an employee of Weil, Gotshal & Manges inadvertently disclosed the identity of the 50 companies that were interested in Global Crossing, a telecoms group forced into chapter 11 protection from creditors. A routine bidding procedure document was sent out to each party. All the e-mail addresses were copied at the top of the document.

It is not often that examples of confidential information come to the public eye. Many organizations take the view that the loss of confidential information is best dealt with privately. However, the loss can be serious, and trusted employees can sometimes be shown to have acted improperly. Consider the case of Carina Coleman, who attended University College, Dublin and graduated with a Bachelor's degree in Business and Legal Studies.

Carina Coleman v Lansdowne Capital Limited & Alan Dargan

Reference for this case: London Central employment tribunal (20 April to 23 May 2003, Case Nos 2201200/201 and 2204067/2001)

Carina Coleman made a number of applications before the tribunal, including unlawful sex discrimination. The members of the tribunal came to the conclusion that there was no unlawful sex discrimination, but the claim for unfair dismissal and victimization succeeded. The members of the tribunal noted the removal of Alan Dargan's confidential list of contacts. The following comments were made in the decision:

> "183 The Applicant described the event as like walking on egg shells. That was consistent with the Applicant's actions next day in removing the Second Respondent's confidential list of contacts. This was an event that only happened to come to light during the hearing as a result of the disclosure order sought by the Applicant in relation to her emails on the First Respondent's system. On one level the fact that the Applicant took the list showed the Tribunal her conviction that she was at risk of being fired and her panic need to assemble information that would help her in her future career.
>
> 184 On another level the Tribunal found naïve, self-centred and not convincing the Applicant's response to this issue in cross examination, asserting she did not believe the list to be confidential. The list was about 100 pages long. Not only did it have names and addresses of the Second Respondent's key business contacts, built up over many years. It also had highly personal and sensitive data such as bank account numbers and PIN numbers.

185 There was also an issue that went to the Applicant's credibility as to whether she took the list off the First Respondent's network system or off the hard disk on Claire O'Dowd's personal computer. The evidence was not clear cut on this technical point. The Tribunal found it implausible that the list would be readily accessible to everyone in the First Respondent's organization, whichever technical steps the Applicant had to take to copy the document and send it to herself at her hotmail address, she must have known, if she had stopped to think, that she was taking confidential information without authority and was doing something wrong."

Tips

- Assess how vulnerable your confidential information and trade secrets are, before establishing an appropriate policy.

- Consider the use of restrictive covenants in your employment policies if some employees have access to trade secrets.

- Check e-mail addresses carefully.

- Employees will send data bases out of the company months before they hand in their notice – what evidence do you have of their wrongdoing?

Breaching the Data Protection Act 1998

With the introduction of the *Data Protection Act 1998*, many organizations are only just beginning to understand the need to ensure documents containing personal data are stored securely. A number of breaches have occurred in the USA. On example occurred in June 2001.

Eli Lilly

Eli Lilly, the pharmaceutical company based in Indiana, manufactures, markets and sells drugs, including the anti-depressant medication Prozac. The company operated a Medi-messenger service, by which a customer could design and receive personal e-mail messages to remind them to refill their medication. On 27 June 2001 an employee of the company created a new computer programme to obtain access to the Medi-messenger subscribers' e-mail addresses and then sent an e-mail informing the recipients that the Medi-messanger service would be terminated. The message included all of the e-mail addresses to which it was addressed in the "To" line, thereby disclosing the e-mail addresses of all 669 subscribers.

Whilst this was an unintentional disclosure, nevertheless the Federal Trade Commission charged Eli Lilly for disclosing sensitive personal information. Eventually, the matter was settled without recourse to a prosecution. The comments made by J. Howard Beales III, Director of the Federal Trade Commission Bureau of Consumer Protection, are instructive:

> "Even the unintentional release of sensitive medical information is a serious breach of consumers' trust. Companies that obtain sensitive information in exchange for a promise to keep it confidential must take appropriate steps to ensure the security of that information."

The office of the Information Commissioner has, to date, taken a "carrot" approach towards ensuring organizations deal with personal data in accordance with the terms of the Act. Although the "stick" approach has been threatened, the number of prosecutions that have been taken, demonstrate this threat has not been carried out. More prosecutions should be considered, especially if sensitive personal data is released, as in the following examples.

>> **University of Montana and psychological records of children**

About 400 pages of documents were accidentally posted on the University of Montana web site on 29 October 2001 and were available for eight days. It is reported that the records of at least 62 children and teenagers were posted on the web site, including complete names, dates of birth and sometimes home addresses and schools they attended, together with the results of psychological testing.

Two significant examples that have occurred in the United Kingdom include Powergen and a subsidiary of HSBC Bank, the details of which are set out below.

>> **Powergen**

When visiting the Powergen web site, John Chamberlain, a freelance IT manager came across the names, addresses and bank card details of up to 7,000 customers of Powergen who paid their electricity, gas and telephone bills on-line. Powergen subsequently paid each person £50 in compensation for this lapse.

HFC Bank

In September 2004, 2,600 holders of the Marbles credit card received an e-mail that was supposed to be sent to each individual with a credit card. However, the e-mail addresses of all those on the distribution list were disclosed to each individual that received the e-mail. The problem was compounded when automatic responses were sent from those addresses that were not responding their e-mails, because the auto response often had the personal contact details of the individual customer included in the e-mail. The bank apologised for the error and admitted the breach to the Information Commissioner.

Some organizations will be more conscious of the issues relating to the protection of personal data than others. Whilst many may be embarrassed if their marketing database is exposed, other organizations should tread more carefully, especially schools and those dealing with medical records. A head teacher will be responsible when personal data relating to their pupils is compromised – a matter of great importance to every parent, bearing in mind politicians are now insisting that all records are sent over the internet.

The comments made by a parent, who declined to be identified, whose child's details were exposed on the University of Montana web site should be borne in mind by every politician that insists every record should be put into electronic format and sent over the internet:

> "He's just a kid, and he shouldn't have his whole life splattered around for the whole world to know....." Recalling the therapist taking notes in her book, the parent "thought maybe that was the extent of it. I guess I was kind of naïve about that."

Politicians are very naïve about requiring all schools to send personal data relating to pupils and members of staff over the internet. Head teachers, members of staff and parents should be aware of this move and take steps to ensure proper security measures are in place to protect the information if the politicians want to play around with sensitive data in this manner.

Using copyright material without permission

The state provides a means of protecting works that are literary, dramatic, musical and artistic by means of copyright. The protection is extended to the means by which the work is produced, such as a sound recording, film, broadcast or cable programme. Copyright also exists in a computer program. As a result, when a visitor visits a web site, their computer will actually download an array of content into the temporary cache (whether copies of photographs, the graphic design of the web site or moving images or games), the content of which will usually be protected by copyright.

It is probably accepted that the act of visiting a web site and downloading content into a temporary cache file is a legitimate use of the content, if only because that is the way one computer passes on information to another computer. However, it is what the recipient does with the copyright material that is important. A person can infringe copyright directly by using the material without permission of the owner in a number of ways (this list is not exhaustive):

- By providing copies of the work to members of the public without permission.

- Renting or lending the work without permission.

- Broadcasting the work, such as putting the copyright work on their own web site and permitting others to download it, without the permission of the copyright owner.

It is also possible for a person to infringe copyright by secondary means. This may well occur where an organization, in the course of business, possesses a copyright article that it knows is an infringing copy. If, in the circumstances, a reasonable person thinks the person or organization knew the copyright material was infringing the ownership rights of the owner of the copyright material, there is evidence of a guilty mind and therefore a liability.

Making statements negligently

The organization can be held liable where advice is offered to a third party where the person receiving the advice can reasonably show they were intended to rely on the advice. Where an employee offers advice by e-mail, for instance, the organization can be liable for the employee's actions in the same way as if the advice was printed in a letter using the organization's stationery. Care should be given to ensure that employee's understand such issues fully, in the same way as they should understand how easily it is possible to enter a contract by way of an exchange of e-mail, instant messages or text messages.

Formation of contract

It is very easy for two parties to enter a contract under English law. It only takes employees of two organizations to exchange e-mails between each other to commit each organization to duties and obligations under a contract. It will not always follow that the employees entered the contract without authority. The point is, where an employee is using the employer's e-mail system, it is probably reasonable for the recipient to assume that the employee has the authority to enter a contract on behalf of the organization.

Elements of a contract

For a contract to be legally binding under English law, the following elements (in outline) must be in place:

- One party must make an offer and the other party must accept the precise offer.

- There must be an intention to enter a legally binding contract.

- The people involved with the formation of the contract must have the capacity to enter the contract (this is where a disclaimer at the end of an e-mail can be effective – by pointing out to the recipient of an e-mail that the person sending the e-mail does not have the authority to bind the employer, for instance).

- Both parties must receive some benefit from the arrangement.

It is perfectly possible for two parties to agree the terms of a commercial arrangement by way of an exchange of e-mails. Even if they intend to enter into a legally binding contract, it does not follow that a contract exists. This could be because the exact terms of the contract have not been agreed, or one or both parties intended the exchange of e-mails to settle the terms of the contract before entering into a separate, written agreement, as in the following example.

Pretty Pictures Sarl v Quixote Films Ltd

Reference for this case: [2003] All ER (D) 303 (Jan)

Facts

James Velaise, through his company, Pretty Pictures Sarl, distributed films in French speaking countries. Quixote Films Ltd is the corporate vehicle for a documentary film, and the three directors of the company were the directors of the film in varying capacities. Quixote Films appointed an experienced film sales agent, Rosa Bosch, to conduct the negotiations for the distribution of the film in France.

Between February 2002 and April 2002 Mr Velaise and Rosa Bosch conducted negotiations, mainly by e-mail. After a number of e-mails had passed between them, Mr Velaise sent the following text to Rosa Bosch on 26 April 2002:

> "Dear Rosa, Further to our today's conversation, here is my revised offer. Licence fee: MG 80,000 Euros; 20,000 upon signature, 80,000 upon delivery. Term: 15 years. Territory: France, French speaking Switzerland, video and paid TV only, Monaco, Domtom, Mauritius, ex-French speaking African colonies. Rights: All rights, all cinema, all video, all TV. Split cinema 50:50, cost off top. Video, 70 us 30 you; TV, 70 us 30 you. All rights crossed. MG deducted from your share."

He ended the e-mail:

> "I hope we now have a deal, and I look forward to your confirmation and receiving a deal memo by fax."

A number of further e-mails passed between the two, discussing the finer points of the deal. In each of his e-mails, Mr Velaise continued to refer to the "deal memo", which he expected would be exchanged and signed between the parties to confirm the contract. Finally, on 7 May 2002, Rosa Bosch sent an e-mail as follows:

> "The deal is approved. Apologies for the delay. You will be receiving the contract by email before commence tomorrow."

A contract was never signed between the parties, and it was claimed by Mr Velaise that this final e-mail sent by Rosa Bosch constituted an unconditional acceptance of his earlier offer.

Decision

Newman J held that the exchange of the e-mails did not show there was a binding contract between the parties. While the exchange of e-mails helped to formulate the basis for an agreement, nevertheless it was abundantly clear that both parties anticipated a legally binding contract would only be formed once a formal document was signed between them.

Every organization should pay particular attention to ensuring employees are trained in the formation of contracts, and internal procedures are adopted to prevent employees from entering contracts unwittingly. For instance, internal e-mails between employees and relevant line supervisors can lead to a variation of an employment contract, as outlined in the following example, which also demonstrates the use of an electronic signature, because typing a name into an e-mail is a form of electronic signature:

Mr J F Hall v Cognos Limited

Reference for this case: Hull industrial tribunal (10 December 1997, Case No 1803325/97)

Facts

Cognos Limited employed Mr Hall as a sales executive. He was provided with a car for business and personal use. Mr Hall was reimbursed for all reasonable expenses incurred for travel, accommodation and other costs in accordance with the relevant policy. The policy stated that all expenses over six months old would not be paid. Mr Hall failed to submit any travel expenses between 1 December 1995 and 3 June 1996.

By January 1997 Mr Hall wanted his expenses paying. A series of e-mails were exchanged on 15 January between Mr Hall, Sarah McGoun and Keith Schroeder, Mr Hall's line manager. Mr Hall asked if the late submission was "OK with you?" and his line manager said, "Yes, it is OK." Mr Hall subsequently submitted his expenses, although he did not provide all the necessary forms immediately. He also inflated his claims. His employers refused to make any payment.

Decision

It was held that the exchange of e-mails between Mr Hall and his line manager varied the contract of employment. The chairman of the tribunal accepted that the printed copies of the e-mails were in writing and signed (the e-mails were signed "Sarah" and "Keith"). As a result, the employer was obliged to pay Mr Hall his reasonable expenses. Both parties subsequently agreed the claim would relate to 9,960 miles at 9 pence per mile, and it was ordered that the employer pay Mr Hall £896.40.

It is important to ensure that employees understand the basic elements of entering a contract, especially whose terms apply to the contract and what, if any, misrepresentations were made in e-mails before the contract was concluded. If suitable training for all members of staff is not considered necessary, this issue should be addressed by establishing a method by which only certain employees have the authority to enter a contract.

There are some rules that employees should follow:

- Be clear by writing accurate, brief and unambiguous prose in plain English. Use simple language and write positively. Do not write using negatives.

- If vague language that is ambiguous is used, it might be construed to the disadvantage of the writer. Use short sentences to avoid being imprecise.

- The text should be logically set out so that both the sender and the recipient know who is responsible for doing what, at what time, how they are going to do it and who will pay.

Discrimination

Networked communications enable people to circulate inappropriate comments that can result in sexual or racial discrimination. In addition, the *Employment Equality (Religion or Belief) Regulations 2003* (SI 2003/1660) and *Employment Equality (Sexual Orientation) Regulations 2003* (SI 2003/1661) make it unlawful for an employer to discriminate on grounds of religion or religious belief and sexual orientation. Both these Regulations are similar in structure to the *Sex Discrimination Act 1975* and the *Race Relations Act 1976*. Discrimination can be direct or indirect, and take the form of victimization or harassment. Employers should also be aware of the provisions of the *Protection from Harassment Act 1997*, which makes it a criminal offence to pursue a course of conduct on at least two occasions that is considered to be harassment, or to cause a person to fear that violence will be used against them. This Act is primarily aimed at stalkers, but can also be used where e-mails cause harassment to employees in the workplace.

There is no qualifying period for in such cases, and compensation is not subject to a maximum limit. An abusive e-mail, for instance, can demonstrate harassment of a sexual, racial, religious or sexual orientation nature, and provide evidence that an employer tolerates such attitudes in the workplace. The employer is liable.

Harassment means unwanted conduct of a personal nature, or other conduct based on sex or racial content that affects the dignity of men and women at work. It is manifest in conduct that is unacceptable, unreasonable and offensive to the recipient. It is a defence in both sexual and racial discrimination cases to show that the organization has taken such steps that are reasonably practical to prevent employees carrying out such acts. To establish this defence, it must be shown that there was proper and adequate staff supervision and publication of the equal opportunities policy, which should refer to the e-mail policy.

The following cases help to illustrate that e-mails in particular can produce evidence of such behaviour.

Sexual discrimination

Please note, when reading through the facts of the case of Mrs J M Bower as set out below, that the matters discussed represent only a part of the totality of evidence put before the members of the tribunal.

Mrs J M Bower v Schroder Securities Limited

Reference for this case: London Central employment tribunal (Hearings throughout 2000, 2001 and 2002, Case No 3203104/99 and 3203104/99/S)

Facts directly affecting the use of e-mail in this case

During the mid-1990s, it was decided internally at Schroder Securities (now Schroder Saloman Smith Barney) that it was important to recruit a new drinks analyst who could cover the European market. In keeping with common practice in the industry, a group of senior people discussed the names of those they knew that they might approach to recruit for such a role. The name of Mrs Bower emerged as a potential candidate, partly because some had read her research, and some knew her.

Mrs Bower had nine years' experience for working in the City. She previously worked for Credit Lyonnais, and from 1994 she was with ABN-Amro, becoming a director in March 1996. Whilst at ABN-Ambro, she built up a team to analyse the two drinks sectors in the UK, covering alcoholic beverages and breweries, pubs and restaurants. Mrs Bower was interested in joining

---

Schroder Securities, and after a series of meetings and discussions about contractual terms, she began working for Schroder on 1 April 1997, leaving on 8 October 1999. Although Mrs Bower's contract directed her to report to Patrick Wellington, Head of UK Research, it transpired that her immediate superior was Michael Crawshaw, Head of European Research.

By October 1997, it became apparent for various reasons that Mr Crawshaw preferred that Mrs Bower did not continue with her employment. Initial evidence for this conclusion was the existence of an e-mail sent by Mr Crawshaw to Rachel Harry in personnel, as follows:

> "Can you tell me what [Mrs Bower's] package is, when bonuses are paid out and what it would cost to pay her off if we need to (unfair dismissal, decided you aren't what we want etc.)."

As time went by, disagreements between Mrs Bower and other people occurred within Schroder. For instance, during the course of April and June 1998 there was a debate, conducted largely by e-mail, as to whether Mrs Bower or Caroline Levy in New York should cover Coca-Cola beverages. Barry Tarasoff was Caroline Levy's line manager. Making Mrs Bower the lead analyst for 12 months, to be reviewed thereafter, concluded the matter. However, by early 1999 it appeared Mr Crawshaw was keen to remove Mrs Bower, evidence for which is demonstrated in an e-mail from him to Mr Tarasoff in New York:

> "I am now managing Julie out of the business. Although she has one or two fans at Schroder's and among the client base, she doesn't get on with many of the people that count. In no particular order of importance: Leon Kalvaria, Rory Maw, Kieran Mahon, Andy Smith, Caroline Levy (me?).

> If she were truly inspirational we might put up with the personality. However, her research is average at best, no target account rates her in their top three, commission figures are low, and her standing with the sales force is the lowest of any senior analyst.

I told her to buck up in her mid-year appraisal. In the end-year appraisal just gone I told her that she was dramatically under-performing the other analysts and that her relationships with colleagues were poor. Her bonus is getting slashed in a fortnight and then she will probably leave and/or I'll ask her to leave (I don't want to fire someone just before bonus round, and in any case, she does still deserve some small bonus.)

We shall then be looking to replace her and get Caroline involved in the process."

On the same day, Mr Crawshaw also sent an e-mail to Philip Kay, Head of Japan, the content of which indicated Mr Bower would not remain an employee of Schroder's for long:

"I wouldn't factor a global brewing piece into your plans."

A further dispute about what areas of stock Mrs Bower covered arose in August 1999 in connection with the coverage of Bass. Matters came to a head when Jean-Baptiste Delabare, the leisure analyst and Head of French Research made an enquiry of Mrs Bower. Mrs Bower saw this request as an attack on what areas of stock she covered. As a result, she replied to Mr Delabare's request (which he sent by e-mail), and included the following:

"I have launched an official grievance against the management of Schroder's to uphold my contract, a situation with which the chairman of Schroder's is now involved. At this stage, therefore, my position is that the Paris office will not cover, write on, or meet with these companies (i.e. Bass, Compass and LVMH) until further notice."

Mrs Bower sent copies of this response to Mr Crawshaw, amongst others. Mr Crawshaw responded by sending a copy of a note to most of the people that received Mrs Bower's e-mail, as follows:

"Julie has gone too far this time. I have prepared the pack of supporting evidence for Julie's dismissal and will circulate it later today."

This response was sent within three hours of Mrs Bower's e-mail to Mr Delabare. As a result of this exchange of e-mails, Schroder's initiated a formal disciplinary procedure against Mrs Bower, at the end of which Mrs Bower resigned, her notice expiring on 8 October 1999.

Decision

The members of the tribunal concluded that Mrs Bower's claim for unfair dismissal succeeded. In respect to her claims for unlawful sex discrimination and equal pay, it was determined that the claim was successful in respect of the 1998 bonus and succeeded as a sex discrimination claim in respect of dismissal. The members of the tribunal came to this decision party because of the evidence adduced in the form of the e-mails set out above. The members of the tribunal said of the e-mail Mr Crawshaw sent in response to Mrs Bower's e-mail to Mr Delabare "We agree with the Applicant [Mrs Bower] that he [Mr Crawshaw] must have been collecting evidence in support of her dismissal over the previous few months, which is why he was able to react so promptly."

An important aspect of the findings of the members of the tribunal in this case is that they found from the evidence that they heard and read, that "Her [Mrs Bower's] tone in e-mails and other correspondence demonstrated increasing non-cooperation and anger as the plots which she perceived seemed to thicken around her. However, her fears, anxieties and suspicions were well-placed in respect of Mr Crawshaw and we are satisfied that she would have behaved differently if she had been nurtured and supported by him (as were the comparators) rather than undermined."

The claim failed in respect to the bonus for 1997; the failure to be promoted to director in April 1999 and as an equal pay claim in respect of a £1.5m bonus and potential entry to the partnership plan which became terms of the comparator's contracts in June 1999.

Mrs Bower was awarded: £740 net compensation for unfair dismissal and £1,414,619.65 net (inclusive of interest) in respect of unlawful acts of sex discrimination.

In matters relating to such issues, the employer must make it explicit to employees that:

- Personal comments, including humour and sarcasm, should not be included in any e-mail.

- Employees have a duty to forward any e-mail that appears to be discriminatory or offensive to the appropriate authority within the organization.

- E-mails containing such material will attract disciplinary proceedings.

Note the case of *Virdi v The Commissioner of Police of the Metropolis* mentioned elsewhere in this book, and the size of the damages that the police were ordered to pay Mr Virdi. A more recent illustration of the appalling behaviour of some employees is illustrated by the case set out below.

Holden Meehan Financial Services

A 37 year old sales support administrator and personal assistant discovered that nine of her colleagues had circulated e-mails about her. She inadvertently discovered about 40 e-mails after she was given access to the computer of a colleague whilst he was on extended leave. The content of the e-mails were described as including matters of a sexual and violent nature. A complain was made to her employer, but she resigned, because she claimed her complaint was not taken seriously. She prepared to take a case of constructive dismissal and sexual harassment before an employment tribunal. After making her complaint, she claimed she was ostracised by her colleagues. Astoundingly, the office manager is alleged to have commented to her "Imagine how the others feel, some of them are losing their jobs" making it appear that she was to blame for the possibility that some people might lose their jobs – the very people who initiated the unpleasant e-mails about her! The company was taken over by Bradford & Bingley in June 2003. The matter was settled before reaching the tribunal, and a payment of £10,000 in compensation was made to her in August 2003.

Racial discrimination

Evidence of direct discrimination can be difficult to obtain in some instances, but with e-mail, the intentions of individuals can be readily observed, as the following case demonstrates.

Mr Khalid Jayyosi v Daimler Chrysler Limited

Reference for this case: Bedford employment tribunal (Hearings in February and March 2003, Case No 1201592/02)

Facts

Mr Jayyosi is of Palestinian origin and is a national of Bahrain. He was resident in the United Kingdom as an asylum seeker. The state provided him with a document indicating there were no restrictions on his entitlement to work. Mr Jayyosi was skilled in the use of computers and information technology and has a Diploma in Business Management. He had worked for a number of companies before taking up employment with Daimler Chrysler on 8 August 2001, after attending three selection interviews. Daimler Chrysler knew Mr Jayyosi was an asylum seeker when the decision was made to offer him full-time employment.

In December 2001, Mr Jayyosi received an appraisal from his line manager, Mr Iain Moulson. He was marked "above target" (the highest rating) in all three areas mentioned in the appraisal: individual performance, values and overall performance rating. Although Mr Moulson had concerns about Mr Jayyosi being late on occasions, this was the only criticism.

Mr Jayyosi sent an e-mail dated 25 February 2001 to Mr David Werner, the Human Resources Manager, asking him to support his application for asylum by writing a letter on his behalf. One of the reasons Mr Jayyosi had for submitting such an application at this stage concerned his inability to attend meetings in Germany on behalf of the company. His permit restricted his movements to within the United Kingdom. Mr Werner sent on the request by Mr Jayyosi to Michelle Thubron, a Human Resources Specialist. Ms Thubron was required to discuss the request with Mr Jayyosi and deal with it on behalf of the Human Resources Department.

Ms Thubron met Mr Jayyosi on 27 February 2002, and she gave him the impression, during the course of this meeting, that she was suspicious of him. On 1 March 2002, Ms Thubron sent a note of her meeting to Mr Werner and Mr Moulson. The content of this note indicated her "concern" about the request, and raised a number of points, including:

> Whether to accept what Mr Jayyosi said "at face value or consider the issue in greater detail to make sure there isn't any doggieness."

> She also asked, "how critical an employee is Khalid".

Ms Thubron subsequently sent an e-mail to Mr Werner on 26 March 2002. She noted there was to be a meeting with Mr Moulson and Mr Meacham (the Support Services Team Leader) on 9 April 2002, and spoke of the need to ensure Mr Moulson should be made aware of "exiting" Mr Jayyosi. The content of the e-mail went on to suggest that Mr Jayyosi had not been performing as required, and continued:

> "Equally Iain has a few other concerns regarding Mr Jayyosi and you are aware of my concerns regarding Mr Jayyoshi's

request for DCUK to help him with the passport .... [It was her view that they should not] ...go down the disciplinary route especially as Iain gave Mr Jayyosi an exceeded appraisal in 2001, and this might leave us open to Mr Jayyosi using the 'race' card if he is dismissed on performance issues ... I don't want to get close to Khalid having 1 year service ... And Khalid will continually ask what DCUK can do towards helping him with his passport."

On 28 June 2002 Mr Jayyosi was dismissed with immediate effect, ostensibly because he was being made redundant, although the new job description was almost identical to his previous job description. In their defence, Daimler Chrysler claimed that, as a matter of routine, they dismiss employees they no longer wish to employ and who have worked for the company for less than a year. The members of the tribunal made the comment that "This was said shamelessly."

Decision

The members of the tribunal concluded that Mr Jayyosi was dismissed on racial grounds, and the following comments were also made in the decision:

- Ms Thubron was the first to raise 'race' as a possible issue, and the e-mail she sent demonstrated the intention to dismiss Mr Jayyosi before it was decided how to effect his dismissal. The members of the tribunal described the redundancy process as "a sham". They also noted that, given Mr Thubron's position, her use of language, such as 'we knew he was ethnic,' was surprising.

- Mr Jayyosi was also subject to other examples of racial abuse, which he encountered during the period he was employed.

- Daimler Chrysler failed to demonstrate any "clear and demonstrable commitment to equality of opportunity." The company only had a policy consisting of a single paragraph, without any guidance as to the meaning of discrimination or how the policy should be applied. The company had provided no training, and it was commented that Ms Thubron lacked a thorough grasp of the Race Relations Act.

Mr Jayyosi was awarded: £30,763.53 for past loss; £35,283.70 for one year's future loss of earnings; £12,913.84 (this sum includes interest) for injury to feelings in respect of unlawful acts of racial discrimination.

Daimler Chrysler UK Limited was also ordered to provide Mr Jayyosi with:

- An unequivocal apology for the race discrimination that he was subject to and which the employment tribunal found he was subject to. The members of the employment tribunal required Daimler Chrysler to provide the apology by a person in a senior management position within the company.

- A reference that stated that Mr Jayyosi was dismissed on racial grounds and that an employment tribunal so found.

Criminal offences

In all probability, criminal offences were committed by way of e-mail as soon as the facility became available. However, examples that exist in the public domain of such activity are rare, because organizations tend to deal with such matters in confidence without reporting the offence to the authorities. In the case illustrated below, there is no record of the police taking any action against the employee concerned. However, the case does illustrate how employees can misuse the communication infrastructure and the type of response they might offer for their behaviour.

Mr H F Miseroy v Barclays Bank plc

Reference for this case: Bedford employment tribunal (18 March 2003, Case No 1201894/2002)

Facts

Mr Hilary Miseroy was employed by Barclaycard in the Fraud Prevention Department between 14 March 1988 and 13 September 2002. The Staff Manual dated 16 June 2000 included a policy in relation to the supply and trafficking of drugs and money laundering. In addition, the Group IT Security Policies, dated July 2002, included instructions about the use of the corporate e-mail facilities. Clear guidance was set out by Barclays in both these areas.

In July 2002, Maureen Crane, a Senior Fraud Analyst, was informed that an individual within her team appeared to be receiving a disproportionate number of e-mails during the day. A formal investigation was subsequently initiated. The Information, Risk and Security Department carried out an audit of the e-mails sent and received by three employees. The audit indicated that Mr Miseroy sent a significant number of e-mails. As a result, he was also included in the investigation.

After a series of investigatory meetings, it was concluded that Mr Miseroy had abused the e-mail facilities, as follows:

*   He sent out an unwarranted number of personal e-mails. On some days eight or more exchanges had taken place in quick succession.

*   Some of the e-mails he sent out included content that was derogatory, offensive and sexist. During his first interview, he accepted that the comments he made were not appropriate. Later, he contended that there was a great deal of social activity and laddish banter between

employees working within the Fraud Department and he did not consider that anybody had been offended.

- A number of e-mails were exchanged between him and Andrew West, a manager in a different department, between 26 April and 30 April 2002. The content of these e-mails referred to the purchase of cannabis from a friend of Mr Miseroy, who in turn passed the drug to Mr West. Similar e-mails had been passed between Mr Miseroy and Mr West between 15 February and 10 April 2002. In an e-mail dated 15 February, Mr Miseroy wrote to Mr West:

  "I've brought it in with me. Fag-break about 10.30?"

- In a further e-mail sent on 18 February, Mr Miseroy asked "quality ok?"

- It was also determined that Mr Miseroy disclosed confidential information regarding Barclay's operations and customers.

Mr Miseroy was summarily dismissed for gross misconduct on 13 September 2002. In his defence, Mr Miseroy maintained he was treated differently from Mr West, who was given a final written warning. However, the following factors did not help his case:

- Mr Miseroy faced a greater number of charges than Mr West relating to the transmission of inappropriate e-mails.

- He lied at the first investigatory meeting.

- It was Mr Miseroy who supplied drugs on Barclay's premises, not Mr West.

- Mr West was remorseful and contrite in responding to the charge made against him, and provided explanations for his behaviour.

- Mr Miseroy did not accept that he was wrong in sending out e-mails with content that was inappropriate. Further, he did not seem to accept that his e-mails relating to the supply of cannabis represented a serious threat to the reputation of Barclays Bank. When he appealed internally against the decision to dismiss him, Mr Miseroy argued about the future classification of cannabis as a Class C drug and discussed whether it was possible for him to enter a binding contract for the sale of cannabis by means of an exchange of e-mails. Such explanations led Mr Tim Kiy, the Marketing Director of Barclaycard Corporate who heard Mr Miseroy's appeal, to conclude that Mr Miseroy failed to understand the reputational risk that his actions posed for the company.

Decision

The members of the tribunal accepted that the dismissal of Mr Miseroy was within the range of reasonable responses of a reasonable employer in relation to the circumstances of the case.

Transmitting and introducing viruses

If the organization sends an e-mail with a virus attached, and causes the recipients system to collapse for a number of hours, it can be argued by the recipient that the sender was negligent in sending the virus. It may be, in the absence of a decision by a judge on this issue, that the sender has a duty to ensure the e-mail and documents it sends over the internet are free from viruses or similar disabling programs.

It appears that attitudes to viruses vary according to the industry sector, according to MessageLabs (www.messagelabs.com), the e-mail security company. Although their press release is dated 9 September 2002, and it appears that no further up-dates have been provided, it was revealed that the retail sector received the most viruses from incoming e-mails, as follows:

Sector	Ratio of viruses to e-mails received
Retail	1 in 24
Leisure	1 in 58

Sports and Entertainment	1 in 68
Building and Construction	1 in 103
City and Local Government	1 in 104
Transport	1 in 107
Charities	1 in 244
IT and Telecommunications	1 in 356
Education and LEAs	1 in 504
Health Authorities	1 in 595
Marketing, Media and Publishing	1 in 658
Manufacturing and Engineering	1 in 1,279
Accounting	1 in 1,789
Government	1 in 2,369
Legal	1 in 2,658
Finance and Banking	1 in 5,208

Where a virus is received, the recipient is under a duty to mitigate any loss. As a result, because viruses are a well-known problem relating to the use of the internet, the organization receiving the virus will have to demonstrate that they took all steps to mitigate their loss. If the recipient fails to protect their system from viruses, therefore, the actual loss that may be recovered will be low.

> **Every organization using the internet and e-mail should have anti-virus software in place to protect their system.**

Employees should also understand that downloading or introducing unauthorized software to the system could cause a system to collapse for various reasons, including the introduction of a virus. In the example below, although Mr Gale was found to have been unfairly dismissed, employees should be made aware that if their actions result in the introduction of viruses, they could face disciplinary proceedings.

Mr P J Gale v Parknotts Limited

Reference for this case: Leeds industrial tribunal (25 March 1996, Case No 72487/95)

Facts

Mr Gale was employed as a Quality Control Manager by Parknotts Limited from 13 July 1992 to 8 November 1995. Soon after Mr Gale began his employment, there were problems about the materials he installed on the computer. It was discovered that the computer was taking far too long to back up information. As a result, a software expert was called in and established that Mr Gale had installed unauthorized software. Mr Nix, the director, gave him a warning in February or March 1993. It was not disputed that Mr Gale worked very hard after this warning.

Further problems were discovered during the course of 1995. It transpired that the entire system had been infected by a virus and was in imminent danger of total collapse. The virus was tracked back to a games program introduced by Mr Gale before Mr Nix gave him the warning. There was no evidence to indicate that Mr Gale had misused the system after he received the warning. Mr Gale was subsequently dismissed after a short investigation.

Decision

The members of the tribunal decided that it was unfair to dismiss Mr Gale because there was no evidence to show he did anything incompatible after receiving the warning in 1993. Mr Gale was awarded a total of £3,810 in compensation.

Falsification of e-mail addresses

The falsification of an e-mail address is known as "spoofing". This is a technique used by people perpetrating a hoax, hackers and people who send out unsolicited e-mail messages (spammers). The aim is to hide the true identify of the originator of the e-mail. Death threats, hate mail, the call to political action and other controversial messages are regularly sent by e-mail that hides the true identity of the sender. Identifying the person that sends spoof e-mail can be difficult, because the origins of an e-mail, which can be found by reading the detailed part of the header, can be hidden or partly hidden. If a person is determined that the recipient does not find out their true identity, the information in the header can be made up using freely available software that is used by people who send spam or junk e-mail. One example is to be found at http://www.mischiefmail.com.

For instance, in the latter part of 2000, the University of Portsmouth was reported to have such a problem. It received over 2,500 complaints from users of Microsoft's Hotmail service in respect of unsolicited e-mails referring them to an adult web site. Superficially, the e-mails looked as if the University had sent them. The header indicated that the e-mail originated from a PSINet dial-up account, with the University as the reply address. Apparently ten other universities were affected in the same way.

In March 2003 silicon.com reported an e-mail sent as a hoax to thousands of addresses that caused a great deal of damage. Somebody sent an e-mail that read:

"If you want to raise a Civil Court action against someone anywhere in Scotland then I am your man. I am a ruthless bastard and I will screw the opposition to the wall even if it means bending a few rules."

The e-mail was purported to have been written and sent by a partner in the law firm Blackadders, based in Dundee. The e-mail contained a signature that included the correct telephone number, name and e-mail address. The firm informed the Tayside police, and the IT department worked closely with the police in an attempt to trace the perpetrator, who used a Hotmail address. Scott Williamson, a partner at Blackadder responsible for IT, is reported to have told silicon.com "What's scary is how this was so easy to do. Any business affected by this kind of thing must realise the ongoing implications".

It is a matter of conjecture as to why such an unpleasant attack on the firm's reputation was executed. However, this problem is a matter for every organization to be aware of, because a single individual can disrupt an organization very easily.

CHAPTER 4
MONITORING NETWORKED COMMUNICATIONS

> **Consider whether there is a better solution to the problem of misuse than intercepting and monitoring**

It can be stated with a reasonable degree of certainty, that it is generally unlawful for communications to be intercepted. The *Regulation of Investigatory Powers Act 2000* makes it unlawful for communications to be intercepted, unless:

- A warrant has been authorized by an approved authority.

- An existing statutory power is used to obtain stored communications.

- The reason is governed by the *Telecommunications (Lawful Business Practice)(Interception of Communications) Regulations 2000*.

- Both the sender and recipient (or the intended recipient) explicitly consent to the interception.

"Communications" include telephones, e-mail, internet and instant messaging facilities in the workplace, provided they are connected to the public telecommunications system.

Communications can be intercepted

By the *Telecommunications (Lawful Business Practice)(Interception of Communications) Regulations 2000* (S.I. 2000 No. 2699), which came into force on 24 October 2000, employers can intercept communications on their telecoms systems. However, if an organization decides to monitor or record communications, it must do so in line with the requirements of the regulations.

Monitoring is permitted in the following circumstances

Users must be informed

An organization can monitor or record communications on their telecoms systems without consent, provided that all reasonable efforts have been made to inform every person who may use the system that their communications may be intercepted. Employees and third parties must be informed that the monitoring or recording communications (which can include telephone calls, the sending and receiving of e-mails, instant messages and use of the internet) is taking place. Should the organization decide to monitor, it is important to have evidence to prove employees and contractors have been informed that their communications will be subject to monitoring.

There must be a business purpose

Where a communication is intercepted in the course of transmission, it must be relevant to the business. A communication that is relevant to a business is defined in regulation 2(b) as follows:

'a communication –

by means of which a transaction is entered into in the course of that business, or

which otherwise relates to that business, or

a communication which otherwise takes place in the course of the carrying out of that business;'

This definition is quite wide, because it covers communications that:

• Are entered into in the normal course of running a business.

• Relate to the business in some other way.

- Take place as a result of running the business other than communications that are entered into in the normal course of running a business.

The relevance of this definition is important. For instance, where a communication is clearly private and not related to the employer's business, it does not appear to come within the definition of a communication that is relevant to the business, unless the organization has prohibited employees from using e-mail and instant messaging for personal and private purposes. Where the communication has breached the policy by, for example, sending confidential information or pornography, then the communication becomes relevant to the business because it is in breach of the policy.

It is important to ensure that a policy is in place that makes the position clear. Where an employee is informed that all communications are subject to being monitored, if they then decide to use the communications infrastructure for private purposes, they are aware of what is taking place and the reasons for the monitoring. If the organization fails to have a policy in place and permits the use of e-mail and other forms of communications for private purposes, then it is highly likely that the employee will have good grounds to object to the monitoring of their personal communications under the provisions of the European Convention on Human Rights and the *Human Rights Act 1998*. This principle is reinforced by the following example.

Halford v United Kingdom

References for this case: (1977) EHRR 523, ECHR; [1997] IRLR 471

Facts

Ms Halford was the Assistant Chief Constable of Merseyside. She made a complaint of sex discrimination against her employer because of lack of promotion. During the course of the investigation, she discovered the telephone provided by her employer for her personal use was tapped. Ms Halford took her case to the European Court of Human Rights and claimed that her employer had breached her right to privacy under

Article 8 of the European Convention on Human Rights by intercepting her calls without her knowledge.

Decision

The judges accepted that the interceptions of telephone calls made from work were covered by the notion of 'private life' and 'correspondence' contained in Article 8. It was held that the interception of her calls without her knowledge breached her rights. Ms Halford was awarded £10,000 including expenses and costs.

Monitoring or recording communications

Regulation 3(1) authorizes the monitoring or recording of communications for the following purposes:

to establish the existence of facts relevant to a business (3(1)(a)(i)(aa))

For instance, this may include keeping records of share transactions or e-mail and instant messages relating to entering a contract.

to ascertain compliance with regulatory or self-regulatory practices or procedures relevant to the business (3(1)(a)(i)(bb))

This includes the monitoring of communications to ensure, for instance, that employees are complying with either external or internal regulatory rules or guidelines.

to ascertain or demonstrate standards which are or ought to be achieved by persons using the system (3(1)(a)(i)(cc))

It is possible, for instance, to monitor to provide for quality control or staff training. Employees working in a call centre may well benefit through having their initial calls monitored to enable them to have feedback on their performance.

in the interests of national security (3(1)(a)(ii))

to prevent or detect crime (3(1)(a)(iii))

If fraud or corruption is suspected, monitoring can take place to ascertain any facts in relation to such a crime.

to investigate or detect the unauthorised use of telecommunications systems (3(1)(a)(iv))

It is possible to monitor to ensure employees do not breach company rules or policies on the use of e-mail, instant messaging or the internet.

to ensure the effective operation of the system (3(1)(a)(v))

This permits the organization to monitor for viruses or other threats to the system.

Monitoring but not recording

An organization is also authorized to monitor communications on their systems in the following cases:

for the purpose of determining whether or not the communications are relevant to the business (regulation 3(1)(b))

The employer can check e-mail accounts to read business communications when an employee is absent.

for the purpose of monitoring communications to a confidential anonymous counselling or support helpline (regulation 3(1)(c))

This covers calls to confidential or welfare helplines to protect or support helpline staff.

Monitoring and employees

The Information Commissioner has now produced Part 3 of the Employment Practices Data Protection Code. This is turn is published in two parts "Monitoring at work" and "Monitoring at work Supplementary Guidance", copies are available to download from the Information Commissioner's web site under "Codes of Practice". A short paper entitled "Guidance for Small Businesses" has also been drafted. The Code covers two types of monitoring, as defined in the Code:

Systematic monitoring: This is where the employer monitors all workers or particular groups of workers as a matter of routine, perhaps by using an electronic system to scan all e-mail messages.

Occasional monitoring: This is where the employer introduces monitoring as a short term measure in response to a particular problem or need, for example by keeping a watch on the e-mail or instant messages sent by a worker suspected of racial harassment.

The aim of the Code is to help employers comply with the provisions of the *Data Protection Act 1998* and to encourage the adoption of good practice. The Code has been issued under s51 of the Act, which requires the Information Commissioner to promote good practice, including compliance with the requirements of the Act. The document sets out the following benefits that will become apparent where an organization follows the Code:

Increase trust in the workplace: there will be transparency about information held on individuals, thus helping to create an open atmosphere where workers have trust and confidence in employment practices.

Encourage good housekeeping: following the Code encourages organisations to dispose of out-of-date information, freeing up both physical and computerised filing systems and making valuable information easier to find.

Protect organisations from legal action: adhering to the Code will help employers to protect themselves from challenges against their data protection practices.

Encourage workers to treat customers' personal data with respect: following the Code will create a general level of awareness of personal data issues, helping to ensure that information about customers is treated properly.

Help organisations to meet other legal requirements: the Code is intended to be consistent with other legislation such as the *Human Rights Act 1998* and the *Regulation of Investigatory Powers Act 2000.*

Assist global businesses to adopt policies and practices which are consistent with similar legislation in other countries: the Code is produced in the light of Directive 95/46/EC of the European Parliament and of the Council of 24 October 1995 on the protection of individuals with regard to the processing of personal data and on the free movement of such data (L 281/31 23.11.95) and ought to be in line with data protection law in other European Union member states.

Help to prevent the illicit use of information by workers: informing workers of the principles of data protection, and the consequences of not complying with the Act, should discourage them from misusing information held by the organisation.

It is recognised that there is a balance to be struck between intrusion and risk to the business. This is why the organization should have a good policy in place.

The Human Rights Act 1998

Where employees are permitted to send and receive personal e-mails or instant messages by the employer, care must be given to ensure there is no expectation of privacy for such communications. Unfortunately, the position is less clear than many would prefer. The *Human Rights Act 1998* implemented the rights set out in the European Convention on Human Rights, a treaty of the Council of Europe, which was ratified by the British government in 1953. The Act allows individuals to take action in domestic courts, rather than going to the European Court of Human Rights in Strasbourg. The nature of the Act is widely misconstrued. Many people think it confers additional rights, especially in the work place. This is not correct. All the Act does is permit people to take action in domestic courts for alleged breaches of rights that existed well before it came into force in 2000. The Act is not an employment law, although some of the rights may apply in the workplace: it enables private individuals to take legal action against a public authority if they consider one of their rights has been infringed. As a result, employees of public authorities can initiate action against their employer for a breach of a right, as defined under the Act. Employees of private organizations do not have the same rights against their employer, although judges are obliged to interpret legislation in a way that is compatible with the European Convention on Human Rights.

Where the organization makes it clear that employees' communications are for the purpose of the business only, may be subject to interception, and such interception and monitoring is carried out within the law (i.e. interception is for a legitimate business reason and is proportionate to the stated purpose), it is unlikely that an employee will have an action against the organization for breach of the right to privacy and correspondence (Article 8). In addition, where the use of e-mail facilities for private communication is forbidden, it can be argued that the organization can intercept personal communications so as to detect unauthorized personal use of the facilities.

However, where the organization permits employees to use the communications infrastructure to send personal messages, interception is prohibited because it will not be related to the purpose of the business. If the organization monitors private communications in such circumstances, it is probable that the employer will be in breach of the right to privacy and correspondence.

The position is made more difficult because of the rights set out in the *Human Rights Act 1998* and the comments made by the Information Commissioner in the relevant Codes, discussed elsewhere. The complication occurs where an organization permits its employees to send and receive personal correspondence, and employees subsequently abuse the resource. Particular care must be taken to ensure the right is circumscribed in the network communications use policy. The aim should be to set parameters by which employees may enjoy the privilege for legitimate personal use only. Employers should take great care to ensure that they have the entitlement to investigate any misuse of the facility by employees who breach the duty of trust and confidence between employee and employer. For instance, the organization should make sure it has the power to intercept and monitor private network communications correspondence where there is sufficient evidence to indicate the employee is using the facility to the employer's detriment. This is because the right to privacy will probably apply to private communications where the organization has given the employee permission to use the infrastructure to send and receive private communications. In essence, the organization needs to take two approaches where personal use of the communications facilities are permitted:

- To ensure employees are aware that monitoring and interception takes place, and it is undertaken within the law.

- To ensure they have the consent of each employee to the monitoring of all communications.

Standards from the Information Commissioner

What the Information Commissioner considers is monitoring

The Code gives examples of what is considered to be monitoring in Section 2, which includes:

- Randomly opening individual worker's e-mails to look for evidence of malpractice. In this instance, the unfairness is manifest. Failure to open a worker's networked communications as set out in the relevant policy will undoubtedly be a breach of the Act.

- Using automated checking software to collect information about workers. An example will be to filter the use of language for particular words to establish whether particular workers are sending or receiving inappropriate e-mails in contravention of the relevant policy.

- Examining logs of web sites visited to check that individual workers are not downloading pornography.

The Information Commissioner has set out the standards in the Code that are expected to be enforced in relation to the monitoring of networked communications.

What the Information Commissioner considers is not monitoring

The Information Commissioner does not consider the following as monitoring:

- Looking back through customer records in the event of a complaint, to check that the customer was given the correct advice.

- Checking a collection of e-mails sent by a particular worker which is stored as a record of transactions, in order to ensure the security of the system or to investigate an allegation of malpractice.

- Looking back through a log of telephone calls made that is kept for billing purposes, to establish whether a worker is suspected of disclosing trade secrets or has been contacting a competitor.

Networked communications can be considered in the same light as paper records. In the paper world, letters, memoranda and scraps of paper with notes of telephone conversations are stored in files. The files are, in turn, placed in filing cabinets. Documents stored electronically are no different to paper documents stored in filing cabinets. If a problem should arise, somebody has to investigate, and they will have to turn to the file in the cabinet just as much as they will have to search the electronic documents to determine what the problem is and how to resolve it. Workers have no rights to prevent employers from reading business documents held in files in filing cabinets, and they have no rights to prevent the employer from doing the same with documents created within the networked communications infrastructure.

The impact assessment

Where the organization decides to monitor, it is crucial to ensure the adverse effects of monitoring are justified by the benefits to the employer and others. For this reason, an 'impact assessment' should be made before monitoring workers. The aim should be to judge whether any monitoring that takes place represents a proportionate response to the problem. The development of the 'impact assessment' involves the following criteria, taken from the Code, each of which is further amplified in the Code:

WHEN MONITORING COMMUNICATIONS, READING EVERY E-MAIL THAT PASSES THROUGH A SYSTEM CAN TAKE SOME TIME.

- Identifying clearly the purpose(s) behind the monitoring arrangement and the benefits it is likely to deliver.

- Identifying any likely adverse impact of the monitoring arrangement

- Considering alternatives to monitoring or different ways in which it might be carried out.

- Taking into account the obligations that arise from monitoring.

- Judging whether monitoring is justified.

The issues to be covered in the impact assessment when considering the monitoring of e-mail are set out in the Supplementary Guidance, at paragraph 3.3.7. The ninth bullet point bears careful consideration, and is reproduced in full below:

> 'Is there a ban on personal use of the e-mail system or a restriction on the types of messages that can be sent? Such a ban or restriction does not in itself justify the employer knowingly opening messages that are clearly personal. However an employer designing monitoring [it is not clear what "employer designing monitoring" means] is entitled to work on the assumption that messages in the system are either all likely to be business ones or, if personal, are only likely to be of a particular type. If personal use is prohibited it may be possible to detect personal messages from the header or address information and take action against the sender or recipient without opening them.'

Further consideration is given to this in paragraph 3.3.8, which states:

> 'Accessing the contents of a worker's personal e-mails or other correspondence will be particularly intrusive. This should be avoided wherever possible. It is particularly important if the worker has a genuine expectation of privacy. This might be confined to e-mails where the words 'private' or 'personal' have been included in the message header if workers have been clearly instructed to mark personal e-mails in this way. If the content of personal e-mails is to be accessed, the employer must have a pressing business need to do so, e.g. grounds to suspect the worker of work-related criminal activity. This must be sufficient to justify the degree of intrusion involved and there must be no reasonable, less intrusive alternative.'

Bearing in mind the increasing numbers of workers that have been detected in sending out confidential information or running businesses from the work place, it seems that this particular point is making two statements:

- First, organizations are, it appears, now required to let employees use the corporate infrastructure to send and receive private communications. It is extraordinary that such a right did not exist with mail sent and received by the organization before the advent of the internet, when correspondence passed through the postal services or by way of facsimile transmission. Organizations would not permit employees to write and send postal correspondence or messages by facsimile transmission at the expense of the organization, so why is e-mail any different?

- Even if an e-mail is marked personal, how is the employer, without opening the e-mail, able to determine whether the worker is sending trade secrets out or distributing pornography (or something much worse), under the cover of personal correspondence? It seems most bizarre that workers can use such a simple device to hide criminal behaviour. It will not always be immediately apparent if a particular worker should be subject to monitoring for criminal behaviour, because such behaviour may only become apparent when another member of staff opens e-mails when the worker is on holiday. Note the case of *Miseroy* v *Barclays Bank plc* mentioned elsewhere in this book, and ask if the investigators would have been able to determine that one of their employees was committing a criminal act without reading the personal e-mails that were exchanged between workers.

Managing data protection in the organization

The text of paragraph 3.1 suggests that complying with the provisions of the Act should be viewed as an integral part of employment practice. The following suggestions have been made to help develop a culture in which respect for private life, data protection, security and confidentiality of personal information is accepted as the norm (taken from the Code):

- Identify the person within the organisation responsible for ensuring that employment policies and procedures comply with the Act and for ensuring that they continue to do so. Put in place a mechanism for checking that procedures are followed in practice.

- Ensure that business areas and individual line managers who process information about workers understand their own responsibility for data protection compliance and if necessary amend their working practices in the light of this.

- Assess what personal information about workers is in existence and who is responsible for it.

- Eliminate the collection of personal information that is irrelevant or excessive to the employment relationship. If sensitive data are collected ensure that a sensitive data condition is satisfied.

- Ensure that all workers are aware how they can be criminally liable if they knowingly or recklessly disclose personal information outside their employer's policies and procedures. Make serious breaches of data protection rules a disciplinary matter.

Tips

- Ensure that your organization has a valid notification in the register of data controllers that relates to the processing of personal information about workers, unless it is exempt from notification.

- Consult workers, and trade unions (or both) or other representatives, about the development and implementation of employment practices and procedures that involve the processing of personal information about workers.

Core principles

The content of paragraph 3.2 of the Code sets out a number of core principles, all of which are elaborated upon in the Code. They are:

- It will usually be intrusive to monitor your workers.

- Workers have legitimate expectations that they can keep their personal lives private and that they are also entitled to a degree of privacy in the work environment.

- If employers wish to monitor their workers, they should be clear about the purpose and satisfied that the particular monitoring arrangement is justified by real benefits that will be delivered.

- Workers should be aware of the nature, extent and reasons for any monitoring, unless (exceptionally) covert monitoring is justified.

- In any event, workers' awareness will influence their expectations.

Monitoring networked communications

The provisions of paragraph 3.3 deals with the issues relating to monitoring communications. The guidelines for monitoring use are set out below:

- If you wish to monitor electronic communications, establish a policy on their use and communicate it to workers. (The features that should be included in the policy are elaborated in the Code). You should set out how the policy is enforced and the penalties that exist for a breach of the policy.

- Ensure that where monitoring involves the interception of a communication, it is not prevented by the provisions of the *Regulation of Investigatory Powers Act 2000.*

- Consider, preferably using an impact assessment, whether any monitoring of electronic communications can be limited to that necessary to ensure the security of the system and whether it can be automated.

- If e-mails and internet access or both are, or are likely to be, monitored, consider, preferably using an impact assessment, whether the benefits justify the effect on the worker. If so, inform workers about the nature and extent of all monitoring of e-mail and use of the internet.

- Wherever possible avoid opening e-mails, especially ones that clearly show they are private or personal.

- If it is necessary to check the e-mail accounts of workers in their absence, make sure that they are aware that this will happen.

- Inform workers of the extent to which information about their use of the internet and e-mail is retained in the system and for how long.

Each of the above recommendations is followed by a number of key points. Some of the key points made in relation to a number of the above recommendations will pose a serious problem to many organizations. It will be very difficult to prevent improper use of the infrastructure if all of these key points are held to be reasonable in the future. The most important are noted below.

Whenever possible avoid opening e-mails, especially ones that clearly show they are private or personal

Key points and possible actions:

- Ensure that e-mail monitoring is confined to address/heading unless it is essential for a valid and defined reason to examine content.

- Encourage workers to mark any personal e-mail as such and encourage them to tell those who write to them to do the same.

- If workers are allowed to obtain access to personal e-mail accounts from the workplace, such e-mails should only be monitored in exceptional circumstances.

If it is necessary to check the e-mail accounts of workers in their absence, make sure that they are aware that this will happen

Key points and possible actions:

- If e-mail accounts need to be checked in the absence of workers, make sure they know this will happen,

- Encourage the use of a marking system to help protect private or personal communications.

- Avoid, where possible, opening e-mails that clearly show they are private or personal communications.

Inform workers of the extent to which information about their internet access and e-mails is retained in the system and for how long

Key points and possible actions:

- Check whether workers are currently aware of the retention period of e-mail and internet usage.

- If it is not already in place, set up a system (e.g. displaying information online or in a communication pack) that informs workers of retention periods.

The issue relating to the retention of e-mails is re-visited in the Supplementary Guidance, where it is stated in paragraph 3.3.11 that "It is important to ensure that workers are aware of retention periods and, in particular, that they are not misled into believing that information will be either deleted or retained when this is not the case." This aspect of the Code will help organizations determine what, if any, software solution they decide to purchase in the future, as discussed later in this book.

Guidance from the European Union

The European Union has established a Data Protection Working Party, and a "Working document on the surveillance of electronic communications in the workplace" (5401/01/EN/Final WP55) was adopted on 29 May 2002. This document makes the following observations in relation to real time surveillance and stored data:

- The employees right of privacy has to be balanced against the right of the employer to control the functioning of the organization and take necessary action to defend any action by an employee that will harm the employer's legitimate interests.

- Any method of surveillance should not be used in such a way as to intrude on the rights and freedoms of employees.

Guidelines are also offered in relation to the general principles of monitoring the use of e-mail and the internet:

- Any action must be necessary, which places a burden on the employer to ensure the purpose of monitoring is absolutely necessary, and traditional methods of supervision are not appropriate. It is accepted that the detection of viruses is a necessary component of any e-mail system, as is the requirement that other employees should be able to read e-mails when an employee is on holiday or out of the office because they are ill.

- Data must be collected for a specified, explicit and legitimate purpose and not processed contrary to those purposes.

- The employer must be transparent about its activities. As a result, the employer has an obligation to inform employees fully about any monitoring undertaken. This includes the provision of an e-mail and internet use policy which is freely available to employees; reasons are given for monitoring; the details of any surveillance undertaken and what enforcement procedures will be taken should the disciplinary code be transgressed.

It must be clear that monitoring must be adequate, relevant and not excessive. As a result, the policy should be specifically written to cover the specific needs of the organization.

Security of personal data

Employers are required to implement appropriate technical and organizational measures to ensure all personal data is held safely and securely against outside attack. The European Union Working Party considers the use of an automated system that opens e-mails automatically is not a violation of employee's rights to privacy, provided appropriate safeguards are put in place. Also, comments were made by the Working Party about the rights that an administrator tends to have on any e-mail system. It is recommended that administrators be placed under a strict duty of professional secrecy with respect to the confidential information they are able to view.

> **Many organizations, including schools, permit employees to have laptop computers. In countless instances, a great deal of personal data is contained on the laptop, including personal appraisals. How many organizations ensure this data, when placed on a laptop, is protected by appropriate encryption?**

Covert monitoring

The Information Commissioner considers the covert monitoring of behaviour can only be justified in very limited circumstances. It is suggested that covert monitoring may be necessary where being open with employees is likely to prejudice the prevention or detection of crime, or the apprehension or prosecution of offenders. The Code sets out guidance for covert monitoring in paragraph 3.5:

- Senior management should normally authorize any covert monitoring. They should satisfy themselves that there are grounds for suspecting criminal activity or equivalent malpractice and that notifying individuals about the monitoring would prejudice its prevention or detection.

- Ensure that any covert monitoring is strictly targeted at obtaining evidence within a set timeframe and that the covert monitoring does not continue after the investigation is complete.

- Do not use covert audio or video monitoring in areas which workers would genuinely and reasonably expect to be private.

- If a private investigator is employed to collect information on workers covertly, make sure there is a contract in place that requires the private investigator to only collect information in a way that satisfies the employer's obligations under the Act.

- Ensure that information obtained through covert monitoring is used only for the prevention or detection of criminal activity or equivalent malpractice. Disregard and, where feasible, delete other information collected in the course of monitoring unless it reveals information that no employer could reasonably be expected to ignore.

The organization should document the above points and only use the covert monitoring for the purpose. The organization should also be aware of the interconnection between the provisions of the *Regulation of Investigatory Powers Act 2000* and the *Anti-Terrorism, Crime and Security Act 2001*, because there may be times when the employer is required to monitor covertly under the provisions of these Acts.

Tips

- Set out the business reasons and benefits for monitoring before deciding to monitor. When assessing the benefits, identify the risks that might be controlled realistically.

- Consider including a specific term in the contract of employment that the employer has the right to monitor and intercept communications.

- The policy should set out when an employee may or may not use the organization's networked communications system for private use. If the policy is not enforced, and a challenge is made in a tribunal, the employer could be held to have implemented the policy arbitrarily.

- Inform third parties at the first available opportunity that e-mails may be monitored.

- Where an organization obtains personal data as the result of monitoring communications, subsequent use of that data must comply with the principles of the Data Protection Act 1998.

- Where there is a clause in the policy relating to monitoring communications, and the organization fails to monitor, monitoring is not possible at a much later stage without a further warning to employees.

CHAPTER 5
WORKERS AND PERSONAL DATA

> The organization must take into account the rights of
> employees in relation to data held about them in
> electronic format

What is personal data

Where e-mails contain personal data (a name on an e-mail is personal
data), workers, ex-workers and competitors can demand to have
copies of the documents held in both manual and computer files that
contain information about them personally. However, just because a
worker sent or received an electronic communication, it does not
mean that they are entitled to receive every communication that they
were party to, as demonstrated by the following case.

Durant v Financial Services Authority

Reference for this case: [2003] EWCA Civ 1746

Mr Durant took legal action against Barclays Bank plc, which
he lost in 1993. In attempting to re-open the claim, he asked
for the disclosure of records in connection with the dispute
that he believed could help his case. To achieve his aim, in
2000 he asked the Financial Services Authority (FSA) to help
him. He wanted to know what documents the FSA had
obtained from Barclays in its role as a supervisory agency to

the banking sector. The FSA conducted an investigation and terminated it without informing Mr Durant of the result, because of its obligation of confidentiality under the provisions of the *Banking Act 1987*. Mr Durant subsequently made a complaint to the FSA Complaints Commissioner. His complaint was dismissed.

Taking the matter one stage further, Mr Durant made two subject access requests to the FSA in September and October 2001. The FSA subsequently provided copies of documents relating to him held in electronic form, the content of which was partly obliterated to prevent the names of others from being revealed. The FSA refused to provide Mr Durant with access to all of the manual files on the basis that the information sought was not "personal" and even if it was, it did not form part of a "relevant filing system". There was no question that some of the relevant files contained information about Mr Durant, including copies of telephone attendance notes, a report of forensic examinations, transcripts of judgments, handwritten notes, internal memoranda, correspondence with Barclays Bank, correspondence with other individuals and correspondence between the FSA and Mr Durant.

Decision

The members of the court of appeal decided a number of questions, and in the context of this discussion, it took a restrictive view of what amounted to personal data. Just because a person's name appears in a document does not mean they have the right to obtain that particular document. Lord Justice Auld gave the judgement, and the following comments from his decision helps to clarify the position:

> 'Mere mention of the data subject in a document held by a data controller does not necessarily amount to his personal data. Whether it does so in any particular instance depends on where it falls in a continuum of relevance or proximity to the data subject as distinct, say, from transactions or matters in which he may have been involved to a greater or lesser degree.'

Lord Justice Auld went on to highlight two issues:

'The first is whether the information is biographical in a significant sense, that is, going beyond the recording of the putative data subject's involvement in a matter or an event that has no personal connotations, a life event in respect of which his privacy could not be said to be compromised. The second is one of focus. The information should have the putative data subject as its focus rather than some other person with whom he may have been involved or some transaction or event in which he may have figured or have had an interest, for example, as in this case, an investigation into some other person's or body's conduct that he may have instigated. In short, it is information that affects his privacy, whether in his personal or family life, business or professional capacity.'

This case has helped to define what is meant by personal data. As the Information Commissioner wrote in the comments made in relation to this case:

'In the Durant case the Court of Appeal did not consider the issue of the identifiability of an individual. This is often the starting point in developing an understanding of personal data. Instead, the Court of Appeal in this case concentrated on the meaning of "relate to" in that definition, identifiability not being an issue in the case.

The Court of Appeal concluded that data will relate to an individual if it: "is information that affects [a person's] privacy, whether in his personal or family life, business or professional capacity". The concept of privacy is therefore clearly central to the definition of personal data. This suggests to the Commissioner that in cases where it is not clear whether information relates to an individual you should take into account whether or not the information in question is capable of having an adverse impact on the individual.'

The comments of Lord Justice Auld, together with the guidance from the Information Commissioner, demonstrate that where an individual's name appears in a document, it will only be considered to be personal data when the name affects the person's privacy. No longer is the mere inclusion of a name in the information sufficient to enable an individual to require the owner to the date to disclose it to them.

For the purposes of the corporate communication system, the two main Principles of the *Data Protection Act 1998* that require particular attention are Principle 5, that "Personal data shall be kept for no longer than is necessary for the purposes for which it is processed" and Principle 7, that "Personal data shall be subject to appropriate technical and organisational measures to protect against unauthorised or unlawful processing and accidental loss, destruction or damage".

> **How many organizations provide for the security and management of personal data on home computers owned by employees, where employees send e-mails and electronic files containing personal data from work to their personal computer at home and back again?**

In August 2002 the Information Commissioner issued "The Employment Practices Data Protection Code for Employment Records". This document forms Part 2 of four parts that make up the complete Code. Whilst employers are required to comply with the *Data Protection Act 1998*, this Code includes benchmarks that are designed to bring about compliance with the Act. Organizations should pay careful attention to the benchmarks and the notes to the benchmarks when implementing their data protection policies.

Security of the communications system

Of particular importance are the security benchmarks from chapter 3, which include the following.

Benchmark 1

Security standards should be applied that take into account the risks of unauthorized access to, accidental loss or destruction of, or damage to, employment records. The note to this benchmark mentions ISO 17799:1995, the Code of Practice for Information

Security Management, which provides guidance and recommendations that, if followed, "should address the main risks".

Benchmark 2

A system of secure controls should be instituted to ensure workers only gain access to employment records where they have a legitimate business need to do so. The note to this benchmark suggests that information about workers should only be made available to those that need to do their job, and rights of access to such information should be made on the basis of need, not seniority.

Benchmark 3

The audit trail capabilities of automated systems to track who obtains access to and amends personal data should be used. The note to this benchmark suggests that where software uses audit trails, the organization should use such facilities to detect unusual patterns of access to personal information. The example given is where one worker obtains access to information more frequently than other workers in a similar position. Given such a situation, the organization should investigate the position and, if necessary, take action to prevent a repetition of such behaviour.

Benchmark 6

In the case of e-mail, technical means should be deployed to provide for security, such as encryption. The note to this benchmark states that the employer "must not" transmit confidential information about a worker by e-mail "without taking appropriate security measures".

THE OFFICE JUNIOR WHO KNEW EVERYTHING ABOUT EVERYBODY BECAUSE SHE FOUND OUT HOW TO GAIN ACCESS TO UNENCRYPTED ELECTRONIC FILES.

Other points to note include:

- Encryption of an e-mail may protect the content in transit, but it is vulnerable to being intercepted before it is sent or when it is received.

- A means must be provided by which e-mails can be deleted permanently.

- Copies of e-mails containing sensitive information received by managers should be held securely, and access to them should be restricted.

- It is important to ensure that when an e-mail is deleted, it is deleted throughout the system, including any back-up storage.

- Access to information about workers held on servers must be restricted, including to IT support staff and, of course, to any outside contractors. Indeed, the IT support staff may be outside contractors.

There is a difficulty in relation to the deletion of information, as IT managers will be aware. A number of problems arise. First, there is the question of the number of copies in existence. It is probable that the same e-mail will exist in sent and received folders, on multiple backup tapes and on the hard drive of each user. Second, there is a difference between deleting an electronic document and expunging it, as opposed to merely deleting it. Careful consideration should be given in how to deal with the provisions of the Code in this respect. The policy should, as far as possible, accurately reflect the way in which deletion (or the act of expunging) takes place in reality. If in doubt, always err on the side of caution, and ensure the policy provides workers with a full explanation of the issues.

It is for the organization to determine how long private networked communications are retained, and the reasons for the policy should be made explicit to workers. Where a worker resigns, the organization may wish to conduct a search of key words to ensure they have not sent out confidential information before leaving. In such circumstances, it may be perfectly reasonable to retain all private communications for up to 90 days and beyond. How long communications are retained will depend on the length of time a worker has been employed, what position they held and the nature of the work they performed. But do not forget to ensure this matter is included in the relevant policy.

Does the law ask too much?

The requirements of Principle 5 places an onerous, albeit not a totally unreasonable, burden on employers to ensure data – especially personal data – is not retained for longer than is necessary. It is doubtful, given the nature of the technology available to date, whether any organization (including that of the office of the Information Commissioner) is abiding by this legal requirement. Unless every individual deletes every personal e-mail they send and receive from the system every day, it will invariably be the case that many hundreds of millions of personal e-mails sent and received by workers in every form of organization, whether public or private, will be stored on back-up tapes. As a result, most, if not every organization in the United Kingdom will be breaking the provisions of Principle 5.

However, even if the technical problems relating to the deletion of personal communications cannot be resolved with technical solutions, it does not prevent the employer from ensuring that the provisions of Principle 7 are complied with to the fullest extent possible. The policy should clearly state:

- What methods are used to store networked communications.

- How long messages are stored.

- The technical shortcomings that prevent the complete deletion of private networked communications.

The organization should also explain to workers what measures are in place to provide for the security of the networked communications. At present, most organizations will have the vast majority of their networked communications (certainly in the form of e-mail) stored on back-up tapes. Back-up tapes in themselves are only designed as a means of restoring the communication system in the even of a catastrophic failure and the loss of all communications. Back-up tapes are a form of insurance to help with business continuity, not an archive. As such, back-up tapes, because they are portable and relatively small, can be easily removed, restored, and replaced by a worker intent on industrial espionage. Back-up tapes are inherently insecure for this very reason, and care must be taken to provide for the physical security of the medium upon which communications are stored.

Workers rights

In chapter 9 of the Code on "Workers access to information about themselves", the Information Commissioner briefly sets out the rights of workers to obtain information about themselves. Where a worker makes a subject access request, the organization has 40 calendar days to provide the relevant information.

It is important to note some of the provisions of this Code. For instance, benchmark 1 refers to the need to deal with requests promptly, and benchmark 7 specifically suggests, when the organization purchases a computerised system, that it ensures "that the system enables you to retrieve all the information relating to an individual worker without difficulty." In addition, the shortcomings of the system will not be a defence for being unable to retrieve information effectively or at all: a problem that is becoming increasingly apparent as the result of the volume of networked communications and the need to disclose such communications in the event of litigation. Interestingly, the Information Commissioner has stated, in a note to benchmark 7, that where a technical solution is poorly adapted or cannot retrieve information effectively or at all, the organization cannot blame the shortcomings of the system as a defence for its failure to respond properly to a subject access request.

Attitudes to e-mails and personal data

The Information Commissioner claims to be active in promoting an understanding of the rights of individuals under the terms of the *Data Protection Act 1998*, as the comments made in successive annual reports assert. However, when the number of people and organizations that are convicted of offences are taken into account, the picture is somewhat different, as the following table illustrates:

	Number of companies or people convicted	Range of fines	Range of costs imposed
Year ending 31 March 2002	11 *Comprising:* 3 directors 4 Individuals 3 companies 1 Local authority	£50–£5,000	£250–£2,600
Year ending 31 March 2003	10 *Comprising:* 3 as manager or directors 4 individuals 2 companies 1 local authority	£500–£3,000	£300–£2,350
Year ending 31 March 2004	8 *Comprising:* 7 individuals 1 company	£150–£1,000 (one individual was fined on ten counts and received 10 fines of £1,000 each)	£100–£5,000

It should be noted that Richard Thomas, the Information Commissioner, set out to be more forceful in dealing with the disdain that some organizations display with respect to the use of personal information. He told Bob Sherwood of the *Financial Times* in an article published on 8 January 2003 that he intended to foster a culture of respect for personal information, and would do so, in his words: "To use the jargon, I'll be talking softly but carrying a big stick." The evidence appears to indicate the 'stick' has hardly been used.

There is a trend developing amongst lawyers acting for workers that have been dismissed to advise their clients to ask their previous employers for copies of personal data before they take action in an employment tribunal. However, such an application may be subject to the provisions of paragraph 7 of Schedule 7 to the Act. Headed "Negotiations", this paragraph reads as follows:

> 'Personal data which consist of records of the intentions of the data controller in relation to any negotiations with the data subject are exempt from the subject information provisions in any case to the extent to which the application of those provisions would likely to prejudice those negotiations.'

The meaning of this paragraph is not entirely clear. The wording seems to suggest the data controller will not be required to deliver up personal data that set out the data controller's intentions towards settling any dispute with the data subject (in most cases the data controller will be the organization). If this is the case, some but not all of a worker's personal data will have to be given up to them should they make a subject access request.

The provisions of the Act can be onerous, but every organization is required to adhere to the requirements of the Act. As the twenty-first century unfolds, it may be easier to control the electronic medium ever more effectively with technical solutions that also help to effect appropriate security and retrieval measures to comply with the Act.

System testing

All systems need testing. Banks, schools and health authorities are amongst those that test their systems at one time or another, and testing a system using personal data must be considered very carefully. The British Standards Institute has produced a set of guidelines, BIP0002:2003 *Guidelines for the use of personal data in systems testing to help organizations avoid breaches of the Data Protection Act 1998*. Consideration should be given to testing systems to help demonstrate the organization took its duties under the Act seriously.

CHAPTER 6
STORING NETWORKED
COMMUNICATIONS

:::
Retention of documents is not an IT responsibility
:::

Networked communications are very popular. It has not taken long for e-mail, laptop computers and personal digital assistants to be linked across the network. All types of organization either use or are expanding the use of networked communications systems. All who use it applaud the speed and efficiency gained by the use of e-mail in particular, although instant messaging is beginning to catch up in popularity. However, the risks attendant upon the failure to provide for the proper retention and disposal of appropriate communications can cause added expense to the organization to such an extent that the cost of resolving problems may be significantly more than the savings of using e-mail. The case below illustrates that even when the organization has an appropriate document retention and disposal policy in place, defending the terms of the policy in legal proceedings may well prove to be an expensive exercise.

> ## *Rolah Ann McCabe* v *British American Tobacco Australia Services Ltd*
>
> **References for this case:** [2002] VSC 73; *British American Tobacco Australia Services Ltd* v *Roxanne Joy Cowell, as representing the estate of Rolah Ann McCabe deceased* [2002] VSCA

Facts

During the autumn of 2001 Rolah McCabe initiated legal action against British American in Australia. Both sides consented to a speedy trial because Mrs McCabe had a life expectancy of months, possibly weeks. The date of the trial was set for 18 February 2002, but a range of pre-trial issues had to be resolved before the trial commenced, in particular the discovery and admissibility of relevant documents from British American, who were reluctant to deliver up certain documents to the other side. The lawyers for Mrs McCabe applied to the judge for British American's defence to be struck out and judgement be entered for her because it was argued that there was no possibility of a fair trial taking place.

For this reason, a hearing concerning these issues started on 30 January 2002 and continued to 1 March 2002. During the course of this hearing, the judge was:

- Provided with volumes of witness statements.

- Given copies of letters and other documents relating to the legal advice offered by a number of firms of lawyers in Australia and England in relation to the British American document retention policy.

- Listened to the evidence of a number of lawyers, senior managers and directors of British American.

The judge considered he had to determine whether Mrs McCabe was able to receive a fair trial. If she could not receive a fair trial, he then had to decide whether judgment be entered against British American. Having heard the evidence, the judge decided that British American:

- Had a document retention and disposal policy, but the original policy and subsequent versions of the policy were intended to permit the destruction of documents relating to British American's knowledge of the health risks of smoking, the addictive qualities of cigarettes and their response to such knowledge.

- Knew there was a possibility of legal action being taken against them at the time the destruction of documents were authorized, but destroyed the documents anyway.

- Destroyed material contained in electronic format on CD Roms, together with evidence of the contents of each CD Rom (which meant it could not be determined what records had been destroyed), even though it would have been possible to retain such records because of the minimal space required for storage purposes.

Decision

The judge concluded that British American subverted the process of discovery with the deliberate intention of denying a fair trial to Mrs McCabe, in that most of the relevant documents were no longer available. He ordered their defence to be struck out and judgment was entered for Mrs McCabe. Damages were later assessed at A$700,000.

Appeal

Members of the Court of Appeal heard an appeal by British American Tobacco during August and September 2002. The decision was handed down on 6 December 2002. The members of the Court of Appeal concluded:

- The evidence did not support the view of the trial judge that the document retention and disposal policy (including the amended versions) represented a deliberate attempt by British American Tobacco to destroy documents relating to its knowledge of the health risks of smoking, the addictive qualities of cigarettes and their response to such knowledge. Every effort had been made to devise a policy that was appropriate.

- There was no evidence to show that the destruction of documents was carried out in the knowledge that legal action may be taken against British American Tobacco at some time in the future. Proper enquiries were made before disposing of documents.

- It was irrelevant that material stored in electronic format on CD Rom was destroyed, given the fact that the original manuscript documents had been destroyed in accordance with the document retention and disposal policy.

It was held that striking out the defence was out of proportion to the issues brought before the judge. The members of the Court of Appeal allowed the appeal by British American Tobacco. The order striking out the defence was set aide, and the judgment given for damages was also set aside. The proceedings as a whole were remitted to the Trial Division of the Supreme Court of Victoria for a new trial.

This case illustrates the need to ensure the organization can justify the retention and disposal policy. Whilst the policy will take shape around operational needs, the various legal requirements must be taken into account to ensure the policy is reasonable, measured and appropriate. The case below indicates that this decision will probably apply in England and Wales.

Douglas, Zeta-Jones and Northern Shell plc v Hello! Limited, Hola SA and others

Reference for this case: [2003] EWHC 55 (Ch) Case number HC0100644

During the preliminary hearings before the trial in the case of the photographs published by *Hello!* magazine of the wedding of Michael Douglas and Catherine Zeta-Jones, the Vice-Chancellor, Mr Justice Lloyd had cause to refer to the case of Mrs McCabe. Mr Justice Lloyd pointed out that there is no English authority in relation to the matters decided in the McCabe case, and he applied the principle set out by the members of the Court of Appeal to the Hello! case. He said, in paragraph 86, that the principle would be applied in English law because the decision of the members of the Court of Appeal in the State of Victoria is persuasive authority (although not binding on the decisions of English judges) and, more importantly, because he considered their decision to be right.

Document retention and disposal

It is neither practical nor necessary to keep every document created in the course of running the business. With the introduction of electronic storage methods, it is possible to retain bulky documents in a fraction of the space that hard copies will occupy. However, now documents are created in electronic format, it is important to ensure the document retention and disposal policy reflects the way in which employees create, alter and manipulate electronic documents. It must be emphasised that any communication in electronic format, whatever the form it takes, is considered to be a document and must be retained in accordance with the laws and regulations that apply to the particular document.

An example from the United States of America is that of J P Morgan Securities Inc, a subsidiary of J P Morgan Chase & Co. In February 2005, the Securities and Exchange Commission (SEC) found that JP Morgan had failed to preserve its business related e-mail communications between 1999 and 2002 for the 3 year period set out in section 17(a) of the Securities Exchange Act 1934 and Rule 17a-4. The firm was ordered to establish e-mail retention procedures that comply with the record keeping requirements. J P Morgan was ordered to pay the SEC US$700,000. Two additional fines, each of US$700,000, were also levied against J P Morgan by the National Association of Securities Dealers, and the New York Stock Exchange.

In all probability, many organizations have not bothered to develop a retention and disposal policy, partly because paper files are just put into filing cabinets and retained for lengthy periods of time. In addition, it is also probable that few people within the organization know who is responsible for the storage and disposal of documents. To a certain extent, this issue has crept up the agenda in most organizations partly because the majority of documents are now not only produced in electronic format, but also because they are stored on the computer and rarely printed out. This has begun to put pressure on the IT department in particular, yet the members of the IT department are not responsible for the retention and disposal policy. In a commercial organization, the responsibility will be with the company secretary or the legal department, and in a public sector organization, the office of the chief executive will have ultimate responsibility for the policy.

The types of document that have to be retained, and how long they need to be retained for, will partly depend on the nature of the business. Some documents created during the course of a business are common to all organizations, and provisions are made in the relevant legislation for the retention of such documents. Further, public finance initiatives often have contracts that require the organization to retain all documents for the length of the contract (say 30 years) plus seven years after the contract expires.

In essence, document retention periods are set against different criteria:

- Retention periods prescribed by law.

- Rules issued by regulatory bodies.

- Best practice.

It should be noted that some Acts of Parliament also create an offence to destroy documents before the time laid down has elapsed, and some industries (such as finance, for instance), are subject to fairly stringent rules determined by a regulator.

Examples of statutory retention periods

Accounting records

By way of example, consider how long records should be retained relating to business accounts. First, by section 222(5) of the *Companies Act 1985*, records relating to company accounts must be retained (subject to the rules made under section 411 of the *Insolvency Act 1986*):

*   In the case of a public company, for a minimum of 6 years from the date they were made.

*   In the case of a private company, for a minimum of 3 years from the date they were made.

A company director or officer of a company is guilty if an offence if they fail to take all reasonable steps to ensure the company complies with the provisions of section 222(5), or intentionally causes the company to fail to retain such records. The penalties are a term of imprisonment of up to a maximum of two years or a fine of up to £5,000 or both.

To complicate matters, the requirements of section 222(5) have to be considered in the light of other factors. For instance, the Inland Revenue may decide to conduct an investigation into a tax liability. By section 20 of the *Taxes Management Act 1970*, a person or business is required to deliver up or make available for inspection all documents in their possession that might reasonably contain information that is relevant to such an investigation.

The problems are compounded when considering the provisions of sections 34 and 36. Section 34 provides that the period for making an assessment for corporation tax is six years from the end of the year to which the assessment relates. However, where the Inland Revenue has reasonable grounds to believe tax has not been paid because of fraudulent or negligent conduct, under section 36, the period can be extended to 21 years after the end of the accounting period to which the investigation relates.

As a result, the statutory period for retaining the main accounting records (what constitutes an accounting record also needs to be considered), can be set out in tabular form for a public company:

	Effective date	Date it is possible to dispose
s 222(5) *Companies Act 1985*	Date record made during tax year 1	End of tax year 6
Assessment under s 34 *Taxes Management Act 1970*	End of tax year 1	End of tax year 7
Investigation of tax liability s 20 *Taxes Management Act 1970*		Beyond year 7: depends if documents are in your possession
Fraudulent or negligent conduct under s 36 *Taxes Management Act 1970*		End of tax year 6, or End of tax year 21: depends if documents are in your possession

Employee records

An employer is required to retain certain documents in accordance with the *Taxes Management Act 1970*. For instance, section 15 requires the employer to retain all papers relating to payments made to employees for six years. Such records include summaries of expenses; payments made on behalf of the employee; payments made that are connected to the business; and details of benefits in kind.

Further, an employer is required, by regulation 55 of *The Income Tax (Employments) Regulations 1993* (SI 1993/744), to produce the records that relate to the calculation of pay. These records must be retained for at least three years after the end of the year to which they relate. The types of document that must be retained include wage sheets, deductions from working sheets, working sheets, certificates (unless such certificates must be sent to an Inspector) and all other relevant records.

Limitation periods

Politicians have enacted legislation to provide cut-off points, beyond which legal action cannot be initiated. This is to ensure an individual or organization does not have a legal liability that stretches out indefinitely. When developing or revising the retention and disposal policy, consideration should be given to the degree of risk the organization is willing to take when deciding how long to retain relevant documents. There is a balance to be struck between the cost of retaining the documents, whether stored electronically or physically, and the comfort of keeping documents. The organization has to assess the risk that it may need to retain documents to defend itself against the threat of litigation, or it may need to retain documents to initiate legal action at some point of time in the future.

Examples of limitation periods

In most cases, there is a limitation on the period of time that can pass beyond which legal proceedings can be initiated. Placing a time limit on the period that can go by before legal proceedings can start encourages certainty, which in turn helps the organization to set a relatively precise date on the retention and disposal of certain types of document.

The relevant statute is the *Limitation Act 1980* (as amended). Some examples to illustrate the effect these limitation periods may have on the retention and disposal policy include:

Actions for breach of contract	6 years from the date of the breach for simple contracts (e.g. informal contracts such as contracts entered into orally or where there is written evidence of the contract, such as an exchange of correspondence) (s. 5)
	12 years if the contract is under seal (s. 8)
Actions in relation to sums you can recover because of statutory provisions	6 years from the date the debt was incurred (s. 9)
Personal injuries arising from negligence	3 years from the cause of action, or
	3 years from the date the injured person became aware that the injury caused by the other party was significant (s 11)
Product liability	10 years from the date of supply (s 11A, introduced by the *Latent Damages Act 1986*)

Although the above examples indicate there is some certainty with respect to the periods of time documents should be retained, section 32 of the *Limitation Act 1980* also provides for the postponement of the start of a limitation period. These are where:

• The person defending the action has acted fraudulently.

• The defending party has deliberately concealed facts that are relevant to a claim.

• The person initiating legal action asks the court for help to rectify the consequences of a mistake that may have been made.

Further, in the case of personal injuries, judges have discretion, under the provisions of section 33, to waive the time limit completely.

The response for electronic documents and networked communications

The reader will readily note that the document retention and disposal policy needs to reflect:

- The type of product or service the organization sells or provides.

- The statutory and regulatory retention periods.

- The fifth data principle of not keeping personal information for longer than is necessary.

- The Information Commissioner's benchmarks relating to the security of e-mails.

- How the organization complies with laws and regulations in accordance with the relevant guides to good corporate governance, which is mainly managed by a series of reports in the United Kingdom, such as the Cadbury Report (1992), Greenbury Report (1995), Hampel Report (1998), the Combined Code, Turnbull Report (1999) and latterly the Higgs Report (2003). In addition, the OCED has also developed a set of 'Principles of Corporate Governance' in 1999 and the Commonwealth Association for Corporate Governance formulated a set of Guidelines in 1999.

- The likelihood of legal action being taken.

- Suitable control and archiving of electronic documents, including e-mails.

Each organization has different requirements, and it is imperative, in the light of the Enron scandal and the British American case above, that due care is given to comply with the legal and statutory duties consistent with keeping retention costs down and providing for the efficient performance of the business.

> **Should HM Customs and Excise decide to visit on a VAT visit, they will require to see every document in hard format, as well as those held in electronic format. Where documents are held in both formats, expect the Inspector to require both versions to be made available.**

Scenario

To understand the need to ensure the document retention and disposal policy deals with the archiving of e-mails appropriately, consider the use to which e-mail is put today:

Some time ago the accounts department decided that all motor mileage claim forms and miscellaneous claim forms would only be available on the company intranet in electronic format. Employees are required to fill in the electronic form online and submit the form to their head of department by adding their electronic signature to the form instead of signing it with a manuscript signature. In turn, the head of department authorizes the claim by affixing their electronic signature to the form and sending it to the accounts department. In the meantime, the accounts department have been sending and receiving invoices electronically for some years now, dealing with any queries by way of e-mail correspondence.

The HR department have decided to require those employees that fill out time sheets in respect of overtime, to submit their claims using the electronic facilities recently installed.

In the main, the company makes its own products and sells direct to retailers. Although the products have a good safety record, there have been the occasional injuries, all of which (to date) have been covered by product liability insurance. The company has recently decided to manufacture a new product. The documentary records relating to the concept, design and testing of the product comprise meetings, memoranda on paper and by way of e-mail, letters and other documents.

Whilst the above scenario does not reflect the use to which technology is put in every organization, nevertheless e-mail facilities have become a significant tool with which employees communicate both internally and externally. In reflecting upon how the corporate e-mail facilities are used, it is conceivable that the organization requires to re-assess how e-mail traffic is dealt with. The scenario set out above illustrates the differing retention requirements of different e-mails. In this case, there is a requirement to retain all:

- Internal e-mails relating to motor mileage claims and miscellaneous claims for 6 years.

- Invoices sent out of the company for a minimum of 7 years.

- Claims for overtime for 3 years.

- Documents relating to current products for up to 10 years from the date of supply.

- Documents relating to the product in development for a period exceeding 10 years to cover product liability.

- Documents relating to any contracts they may have entered by way of exchange of e-mails for a minimum of 6 years, bearing in mind a claim can be made from the date of the breach, which means if the contract is open-ended, the documents must continue to be retained until the contract is terminated.

The above examples could be described as good practice. It may be, as with the British American case above, that the organization is or becomes aware that legal action is possible in the future. Given such knowledge, it is crucial to obtain appropriate legal advice before taking action to dispose of records. If records are destroyed in the knowledge that legal action is possible, a judge may well make adverse inferences against such actions in the event a legal action is initiated, as in the British American case outlined above.

KPMG already does it

The organization should treat electronic records in accordance with the benchmarks set out by the Information Commissioner. For instance, Jonathan Hunt reported in an article "Knowing the e-form means quicker claims" and published on page v in the Business Travel supplement to the Financial Times on 6 December 2002, that KPMG now require employees to fill in their expense forms online, through the internal network. In stipulating to employees that they must submit expenses in this way, it is assumed that KPMG ensured that the system they adopted for this purpose also provides the security and audit trails required by the Information Commissioner.

Dealing with misuse

Many organizations find the implementation of the e-mail policy (which should now be called the network communications use policy) is fraught with complications. If employees are permitted to use the e-mail facilities for private use, obtain access to the internet to gain access to their hotmail account or use instant messaging software, the organization will need a policy that must be enforced in order to rely on its provisions, should it be necessary to take disciplinary action. Having a policy also means offering guidance, including, but not limited to such issues as:

- Differentiating between private and company correspondence.

- Controlling the communication of confidential information.

- Sending or receiving unusually large e-mails or attachments.

- The dangers of propagating computer viruses.

- Preventing the sustained use of e-mails that substantially hinders others in their use of the network.

As any lawyer specialising in employment law will confirm, the numbers of employees disciplined for improper use of e-mail facilities has grown, as has the number of claims made by employees that have been dismissed for misusing the e-mail system. The costs of enforcing the policy can be expensive, and failing to implement the policy properly, by linking it to the disciplinary and grievance policy for instance, leaves many employers no option other than to settle claims with former employees before a tribunal hearing.

Some significant questions

- How is the communications system being used?

- How many computers are linked to the system (laptops, personal digital assistants, mobile telephones, smart telephones, voice over internet)?

- What percentage of the traffic is legitimate business use, and how much is private use by employees?

- Are employees using hotmail, instant messaging and peer-to-peer applications, which can cause security breaches and allows employees to send, receive and distribute material in breach of the use policy?

- If instant messaging is used, is it being recorded? If not, why not?

- How well are members of staff trained in the security issues relating to the use of e-mail, instant messaging and the internet at work?

- Do the filtering solutions actually work?

- Have the effectiveness of the filtering solutions been tested?

- How many Powerpoint files are used to hide pornographic images?

- How many employees use camouflage (www.camouflage.co.uk) to embed images in a file to prevent screening technology picking up the images?

- How much bandwidth is taken up with extraneous, private e-mail communications, including any attachments?

- What is the cost of the private use of the communication system to the organization?

- How many e-mails are sent by an employee to their home e-mail address (or laptop owned by the organization) with classified files attached that contain confidential personal information (such as medical or school records) that are not suitably encrypted, thus permitting the employee (consultant or head teacher, for instance) to work on the files at home before sending the files back to work?

- How are the principles of the *Data Protection Act 1998* enforced where e-mails and electronic documents are sent by employees to their home computer (which the employee owns)?

- How does the organization ensure the home computer belonging to an employee is a safe repository for personal data?

- When an organization receives a subject access request, it is required to provide all the information requested. How does the organization obtain the information about the person making the request that is contained on the home computers of employees?

- Is confidential and secret information relating to the organization sent out by employees to competitors?

- How many e-mails and instant messages are used to communicate with competitors and for what reasons?

- Is confidential information belonging to the organization (such as the database) being used by employees to set up their own business?

- How many employees have been detected running their own business from the organization's infrastructure?

- Is the database secured in accordance with the seventh principle of the *Data Protection Act 1998*?

- Does the organization look at private e-mails sent and received by employees in contravention of the *Data Protection Act 1998*?

- How many e-mails and electronic documents are passing through the communication systems that are encrypted without the knowledge or permission of the organization?

- Who in the organization is responsible for key numbers in accordance with the *Regulation of Investigatory Powers Act 2000*?

- What are the legal risks for the organization if it fails to address these issues?

- What actions should have been taken to reduce the risks, and by whom?

- Who will be found responsible within the organization if it faces the problems that Norwich Union faced in 1997 or Norton Rose in 2000?

Data protection

A further problem that few employers recognise when they permit employees to use the system for private e-mails, are the employer's duties under the provisions of the *Data Protection Act 1998*. If the system does not retain e-mails in a way that makes searches for personal data easy, complying with a request to deliver up all e-mails containing personal data for a named individual can be a lengthy and expensive process. This is an increasing problem for some organizations in respect to subject access requests, but will have a greater effect on those organizations subject to the provisions of the *Freedom of Information Act 2000* and where litigation begins or is threatened.

An added complication when deciding on a suitable e-mail retention policy relates to the fifth data protection principle, which does not permit personal data to be retained for longer than is necessary. This provision is in conflict with many business requirements, and careful consideration must be paid to this issue when revising the policy and deciding how to archive e-mails within the organization. This is because, in an ideal world, private e-mails should not be retained for the same length of time as business e-mails. However, we do not live in a perfect world, and the policy should accurately reflect the technical limitations that the organization is subject to, and make it clear to the employee how long private communications will be retained, together with an outline of the provisions put in place to ensure the information remains secure, as required under the seventh principle.

Long-term storage of documents in electronic format

The long-term storage of documents in electronic format is the subject of a great deal of literature that is not considered in this text, although some useful web sites have been listed in Appendix 3. In any event, the reader should be aware of the need for electronic document management and electronic record management. The type of storage used for digital data will depend on the requirements of the organization, such as microfilm, near line (optical disk and tape) storage, on line and off line storage. Whichever form of storage is chosen, consideration should be given to the 'Code of Practice for Legal Admissibility and Evidential Weight of Information Stored Electronically' DISC PD 0008:1999 and the 'International Code of Practice for Electronic Documents and e-business Transactions' DISC PD 5000-1:2002, both produced by the British Standards Institute, as well as the relevant documents and guidance issued by the Public Records Office.

Helpful text

For further guidance relating to the retention of corporate documents (including health and safety), see the book by Andrew C Hamer, *The ICSA Guide to Document Retention*, (The Institute of Chartered Secretaries and Administrators, 2004)

CHAPTER 7
NETWORKED COMMUNICATIONS
AND EVIDENCE

> **Any storage solution must have sufficiently robust audit trails in place to provide for the evidential weight of the communications stored**

Documents in electronic format can be adduced as evidence in court. As soon as legal proceedings begin or the organization is put on notice that legal proceedings are contemplated, the organization has a duty to the court to preserve every document that is relevant to the claim. The obligation includes documents upon which the organization may rely and any documents that adversely affect their case. Where one party fears the other party may delete relevant communications, they can make an application to a judge for an order that all electronic records, including correspondence conducted by e-mail and instant messaging, be preserved and copies be handed over to the other side.

Should an organization inadvertently destroy any document (whether electronic or otherwise), such an act may adversely affect their legal position. Where documents are deliberately destroyed, proceedings can be taken for contempt of court. There are two issues to consider with respect to all types of evidence, including e-mail:

- Whether the e-mail is admissible (adducing evidence of e-mails in criminal cases may be more difficult than in civil cases or before an employment tribunal).

- If admissible, the next question is what weight is to be given to that evidence, in other words, how convincing is the evidence? Is it authentic (is there an accurate account of the activity, transaction or decision) and accurate and complete (does the evidence demonstrate the document has not been changed since it was created)?

The adversarial procedure of proceedings in court permits both sides to adduce expert evidence, which means if one party relies on particular evidence relating to the misuse of the e-mail system, the evidence they adduce must be of the highest quality and not open to question by the other side.

Bill Gates found out that e-mails could haunt you years after writing them. When cross-examined in court during the anti-trust case against Microsoft, the following exchange took place:

> This part of the cross-examination, which appears in the videotape deposition of Bill Gates, is referring to an e-mail containing the following three lines:

>> "I want to get as much mileage as possible out of our browser and Java relationship here. In other words, a real advantage against Sun and Netscape. Who should AVI be working with? Do we have a clear plan on what we want Apple to do to undermine Sun?"

> In cross-examining Bill Gates, the lawyer was trying to get him to accept he sent this particular e-mail. The lawyer is seeking to demonstrate Bill Gates was actively involved in undertaking activities, which were claimed to be illegal.

> After reading out the text, the lawyer continued with the question: Now, do you have any doubt that when you talk about 'I want to get as much mileage as possible out of our browser and Java relationship here' you're talking about Apple?

> *Answer:* That's what it appears.

> *Question:* Okay. Do you have any recollection of any discussions about the subject matter of this e-mail in or about August of 1997? If the question was confusing, I would be happy to rephrase it, Mr Gates.

> *Answer:* Go ahead.

Question: Did you send this e-mail?

Answer: It appears I did.

In this particular instance, there was no dispute about whether the content of the e-mail was altered from the original sent by Mr Gates. However, this short example illustrates the following points:

- An e-mail can be adduced as evidence in a court case.

- All e-mails do not need to be retained for the same length of time, and many e-mails can be destroyed legitimately.

- Even if an e-mail is destroyed on the sender's computer, copies of it may continue to exist for many years on the computers of those to whom it is sent, but the content can be altered.

The large US investment banks have good reason to ensure e-mails are controlled more effectively in future, as the activities of Eliot Spitzer, the New York state attorney general have demonstrated over the past few years. He published e-mails during the course of his investigation against certain investment banks in 2002 to support his assertion that research analysts wrote reports that were not as independent as they led their clients to believe. The findings by the research analysts were not warranted by the evidence, as demonstrated in part by the e-mails uncovered by Mr Spitzer. By December 2002, ten banks agreed to pay a total of US$900m in fines to settle the matter.

Although it can be demonstrated that an e-mail came from a particular computer, it does not follow that the owner or user of the computer was the author of the e-mail. In the vast majority of disputes, both parties will invariably agree the bundle of documents that an adjudicator is to rely upon in reaching a judgment. However, it is inevitable, given the sheer volume of e-mails that are now passing over the internet, that cases will arise where one party to a dispute will not accept the content of a particularly important e-mail.

For instance, assume two companies through their employees enter into a contract for the supply of goods that must be delivered on a precise date in the future. Assume the goods are delivered late, and the company buying the goods no longer has a use for them after the deadline for delivery was missed. A dispute arises. One of the employees covers their tracks by amending a relevant e-mail in their mailbox. As a result, two versions of the same e-mail exist.

The question then arises, how does each party to the proceedings deal with this matter? Whichever party relies upon the e-mail (in this case both parties rely on the same e-mail, but with different contents) will, in general, have to demonstrate the integrity of their e-mail system to prove their respective e-mail is the authentic document upon which the adjudicator can rely. This can be a costly exercise if the organization does not have a system in place that provides audit trails for e-mail. Reliance on the ability of well-qualified external forensic analysts is expensive. The costs may far outweigh any legal costs in an action, unless it is prolonged.

Issues to consider

From the point of view of adducing evidence, it is important for the following issues to be considered when providing for the integrity of electronic evidence:

- In some instances, it may be important in deciding whether to take legal action, to establish the quality of the evidence with the provision of audit trails to establish whether e-mails were altered and whether they were received and opened by the recipient.

- The quality of evidence is important. In the case of electronic evidence, if there is no suitable audit trail provided by the software, it may be necessary to spend money on expensive expert evidence.

- If forensic evidence is required, a number of issues must be addressed, such as the chain of custody of the evidence (one break in the chain may prevent the evidence from being accepted: for instance, if the investigator forgets to link the burning of the files to CD Rom, it is likely the chain of evidence is broken, and therefore the evidence on the CD Rom will not be acceptable to the adjudicator). In addition, the forensic method used must be demonstrably transparent and extensive, and clear explanations must be offered in evidence by the forensic investigator, including a discussion of the accuracy of process and the content derived from the e-mail system.

- There is a need to prove, under the *Computer Misuse Act 1990*, for instance, that a computer was involved, that a person gained access to a computer without authority, and the person obtaining access knew they were not authorized to obtain access to the computer. This is a time-consuming and expensive process if there is no proper audit trail already installed on the e-mail system.

- Consideration must be given to authentication of the electronic evidence, and the collection of electronic evidence without altering it.

Printing communications or retaining the electronic version

Many organizations print out e-mails and file them in the relevant files in the false assumption that the printed version of the e-mail is a permanent record. There is one significant problem with doing this: either the sender or the recipient can alter the electronic version of the e-mail. If this occurs, the printed version will be different to the electronic version. As a result, if a challenge is made over the authenticity or integrity (or both) of an e-mail, for instance, there are good reasons to ensure the organization can provide the electronic version, not least because it will be the best available evidence, providing it can be demonstrated that the original e-mail has not been altered since it was created or received. Documents in electronic format are very easy to forge and alter, and the printed version is of no value unless the metadata is retained. In the case of many forms of networked communications, the best evidence will probably be the electronic version, depending on the technical method used to provide for the integrity of the document. Below is a list of some of the issues that are relevant:

- Some programs do not allow recipients within the blind carbon copy (BCC) field to be printed, and it may be important to show an e-mail was copied in this way. In addition, BCC's are not shown except on the message sent by the sender.

- The printed version does not include the metadata (data about the data), such as the original author, their title, when the e-mail was written and the number of revisions the e-mail went through. It should also be noted that some programs do not permit the user to print this information either. (To obtain access to this data from Outlook Express, click on 'File' then 'Properties'.)

- Often the printed version of the e-mail is not accurate, because information can be, and usually is, hidden.

- There is often a conflict between an application and a device, such as the printer. This is a common occurrence, and the effect is to prevent data from being printed, such as the existence of attachments and text that may be underlined or in italic.

The metadata

The term metadata refers to the data about data. It is a digest of the structure and subject matter of a resource. The metadata in relation to a piece of paper may be:

- Explicit from perusing the paper itself, such as the title of the document, the date, who wrote it, who received it and where the document is located.

- Implicit, which includes such characteristics as the types of type used, such as bold, underline or italic; perhaps the document is located in a coloured file to denote a particular type of document; labels may also act as pointers to allow the person using the document to deal with it in a particular manner, such as a confidential file, for instance.

With electronic documents, the implicit data needs to be made explicit if it is to be used to help interpret the purpose of the electronic document. Such data can include, and be taken automatically from the originating application software, or supplied by the person that originally created the record.

An electronic record should contain two main types of information:

- The content of the document and its internal structure.

- The metadata, which describes the record and each of the constituent parts.

The short discussion set out above illustrates the main problems an organization may face if challenged by the authenticity of an e-mail. By ensuring the e-mail system is not open to abuse by any user (this includes everybody, including administrators and outside contractors), the probability of being called upon to prove the authenticity of the e-mail will be reduced.

The costs associated with litigation

Delivering up documents because of litigation (a process called "discovery" by lawyers in the United Kingdom), and looking for relevant documents required by the other side, can be a time-consuming and expensive exercise. In the case of Mrs McCabe, his Honour Judge Eames mentioned one case in which British American had to identify 30,000 documents that were relevant to the particular proceedings. Of these, 11,600 documents were relevant or arguably relevant. This particular process of discovery cost around A$2m.

Securing the evidential trail

Networked communications are in their infancy, although the use of such communications has increased so significantly as to cause significant problems of management and storage for IT departments. It may not come as too much of a surprise to some readers of this text that problems have already begun to occur, especially over finding relevant communications, never mind trying to determine whether a particular communication has been altered in some way. Consider the following scenario, if you are a solicitor (or the client of a solicitor):

> "This is the managing partner here." The introduction over, the voice continued, "A client is challenging the content of an agency agreement you prepared last year. Apparently two clauses are illegal, and we are currently investigating our position." The tension in the managing partner's voice was apparent. "Can we prove the integrity of our version to demonstrate these clauses were not included when you drafted the original document?"

Maybe you are an architect:

> "This is the managing partner here." The introduction over, the voice continued, "You recall the bridge that collapsed so dramatically recently? The state investigator now wants to see our

drawings and calculations, because the design is being called into question."

Perhaps you thought you knew what the terms of a contract were:

"This is the company secretary here." The introduction over, the voice continued, "I want you to produce all the documents relating to the banking facility agreed last year, including any e-mails. It appears we are in breach of a condition that I was not aware existed. Get this information to me within the hour."

When a question of this nature was raised with one firm of solicitors, the client backed down when a paper copy of the document was produced. In this instance, as is now frequently the case, the document was sent to the client in electronic format as an attachment to an e-mail. But what if the client was adamant that the written text held on the solicitor's file was not the same version of the document sent to them as an attachment to the e-mail? Lawyers and clients of lawyers should pay particular attention to this issue. There should be sufficient evidence in place to link each act in the production of a document, from the initial instructions to the delivery of the final version.

Exchange of pre-trial papers

There is a good reason why lawyers should apply themselves to securing the evidential trail of electronic documents. A great deal of pre-trial preparation is conducted by electronic means. This means barristers send electronic copies of their advice or opinion and pleadings to instructing solicitors. In addition, witness statements are exchanged between parties electronically. Given the ease with which the content of electronic documents can be altered, it will be increasingly important to have sufficient measures in place to identify when an electronic document has been altered without authority.

Clients should consider this aspect very carefully with their lawyers, as the example below illustrates. Further, consideration should be given to ensuring the organization can establish, when they send out particularly important e-mails:

• That the message was delivered to the recipient.

- The message received by the recipient was the message sent by the organization.

- All the relevant electronic actions are sufficiently designed to provide an effective audit trail.

Submission of fraudulent evidence

The case of *Scholastic, Inc., J. K. Rowling and Time Warner Entertainment Company, L.P.* v *Nancy Stouffer* helps to illustrate the problems that might arise in future.

Scholastic, Inc., J. K. Rowling and Time Warner Entertainment Company, L.P. v Nancy Stouffer

District Judge Allen G Schwartz in the US District Court for the Southern District of New York decided this case on 17 September 2002

Reference for this case: 221 F Supp 2d 425 (SDNY 2002)

Facts

Nancy Stouffer made a number of claims against J K Rowling, the author of the "Harry Potter" books, one of which was the infringement of her intellectual property rights in the words "muggles" and "Larry Potter". She based her case on the submission of at least seven items of falsified evidence. This included altered copies of an advertisement, the text in a play and a book, drawings, a forged invoice and an altered draft of a distribution agreement.

Although this case may appear to be unusual, it demonstrates that some people are willing to take extraordinary steps to pursue a claim. Whilst Scholastic, J. K. Rowling and Time Warner had a good case to defend, they had to go to the expense of proving Nancy Stouffer had fabricated some of the evidence. For instance, an advertisement was adduced as evidence to demonstrate Nancy Stouffer's rights over the word

"Muggles". The advert submitted to the court included the "TM" mark next to "Muggles". However, the "TM" mark did not appear in the advertisement that was actually printed. Scholastic demonstrated that the version submitted to the court could not have been used for the original advert, because the printing technology used in producing the additional words in the forged version was not invented when the advert was first designed and used.

Similarly, Nancy Stouffer submitted a draft copy of a distribution agreement to establish proof of her claims. The agreement she provided to the court contained a list of the booklets that were to be distributed, the third of which was "RAH". However, Scholastic was able to obtain two original copies of this agreement from other sources, and a comparison between these two and the copy put forward by Nancy Stouffer indicated:

The third item on the original documents was "The Land of the Nother-One", not "RAH".

The words "RAH" were not aligned with the other words on the page, clearly indicating somebody had altered the copy in Nancy Stouffer's possession.

Decision

The judge concluded that Nancy Stouffer had "perpetrated a fraud on the Court through her submission of fraudulent documents as well as through her untruthful testimony". The motion for summary judgment by J K Rowling was granted, and Nancy Stouffer's counterclaims and cross claims were dismissed with prejudice, and she was ordered to pay US$50,000 in sanctions and legal costs.

The future for lawyers and their clients

Such attempts to adduce fraudulent evidence before a court are rare. However, it is conceivable, given the ease with which electronic documents can now be manipulated and altered, that attempts will be made in the future to falsify and alter documents before a trial takes place. Imagine what would happen if both parties relied on the same sentence in a witness statement, yet neither lawyer in court had the same version of the sentence in their electronic copy. Consider a recent example:

> Kevin Maguire parked his car in Market Place in Bury town centre, Greater Manchester at 7.15 am on 31 August 2003. He returned at 5 pm to find he had been given a parking ticket at 9.15 am for £30. Normally there were no restrictions on a Sunday, and when he parked his car there were no temporary signs to indicate there were any temporary restrictions in place. There were no signs because the NCP staff did put them up on the previous night. This was because of the likelihood of them being pulled down or damaged by revellers overnight. When Mr Maguire complained to NCP, it was asserted that he had parked illegally and he was sent a photograph of his parked car, which was dated 31 August 2003. Mr Maguire appealed against the parking fine. Gavin Moses changed the date on the photograph from 30 August to 31 August, so that it appeared he had parked illegally. The adjudicator cleared Mr Maguire of parking illegally and awarded him costs. Gavin Moses subsequently entered a plea of guilty when he was prosecuted for perverting the course of justice in early 2005.

To this extent, both lawyers and their clients need to consider some of the following issues when they next upgrade their systems:

- The integrity of the electronic version of each document they create. This means that each change to the document should be noted and audited, both prior to the final version being sent out and when stored in the document management system.

- The electronic version must be identical to the hard copy retained on the client file. This is very difficult to achieve with e-mails, as pointed out previously.

- How to prove a particular version of a document was sent as an attachment to a particular e-mail. There needs to be an evidential trail linking the document to the e-mail in such a way that it can be proved which version of the document was sent as an attachment to the e-mail.

- Following on from the previous point, there must be a link to show the document that was sent as an attachment to an e-mail was the actual document originally prepared for the client and held in the main file.

Technology undoubtedly enables all organizations to provide a better service to their clients and customers than ever before. However, this example highlights the reverse side of the benefits that come with preparing, altering and sending documents in electronic format. Documents can easily be altered, and all users of networked communications need to pay particular attention to ensuring systems are in place to provide for the integrity of the documents they produce.

CHAPTER 8
CONTENT OF THE NETWORKED
COMMUNICATIONS POLICY

> Careful consideration should be given to ensuring the policy is
> brought to the attention of employees and is kept up-to-date

Every organization is urged to have a networked communications
policy in place, to include the use of e-mail, instant messaging and the
internet, as encouraged by the Advisory Conciliation and Arbitration
Service (ACAS) to its "Code of Practice on Disciplinary and Grievance
Procedures" (Third Edition, 2003). It is for the organization to
determine whether the policy becomes a term of employment, and in
making the decision, the issues set out below should be considered.

- Where the e-mail and internet use policy is incorporated into the
  contract: the employer and employee are contractually bound by
  the terms of the policy. If the employer does not abide by the
  terms of the policy, an employee will have a claim for breach of
  contract. When the employer wishes to change the policy at a
  later date, each employee must expressly agree to the changes.

- Where the e-mail and internet use policy in not incorporated into
  the contract: The policy is regarded as a management guideline
  that seeks to indicate the employer's approach to the subject
  matter of the policy. The policy is not contractually enforceable.
  The policy can be changed without the consent of employees.

Whether to incorporate the policy into the contract of employment
or not, it should be made clear whether the policy forms part of the
employees' contract.

The purpose of the policy

Whether employees are permitted to use any form of network communications, including e-mail and internet facilities for personal use or not, an acceptable policy is necessary to provide guidance and advice to employees. The risks that accompany the use of e-mail, instant messaging and the internet at work include:

- The distribution of material that may be considered to lead to sexual and racial harassment.

- Employees abusing the individual's rights to privacy.

- Defamation.

- Time wasting.

- The distribution of obscene material.

- The possibility that employees may enter contracts unwittingly.

- Leakage of confidential information, trade secrets and intellectual property rights.

- Misuse of intellectual property rights belonging to others.

- The introduction of viruses or other damaging software.

> In one company, Waterford Technologies found two people exchanged 195 messages in one day; in another company, three conversation pairs represented 68 per cent of the internal e-mail, and in one case, 98 messages were exchanged between two members of staff in 90 minutes.

The policy should seek to:

- Educate employees as to why a policy is necessary and aim to regulate their conduct in relation to the use of network communications.

- Reduce the liability to the organization and to protect the employee.

- Ensure employees know what the likely penalties are for misuse of the communication facilities.

The policy and rules

The size and type of organization will determine the how comprehensive the networked communications policy should be. Some or all of the subject areas set out in this chapter may have a place in the organization.

A general policy covering the use of the internet, instant messaging and e-mail facilities, including guidelines relating to security of the organization's intellectual property, databases and confidential documents is essential, regardless of the size of organization. Depending on the size of the organization and the extent of the policy, it may be necessary to split the policy into discrete parts that are easily digestible. A policy in relation to "whistleblowing" and bullying should also be strongly considered, because e-mail in particular can be used to bully.

Guidelines

It should be made clear to employees the extent to which they may use e-mail, instant messaging and the internet, if they are permitted to use these facilities for personal use. In addition, it is also useful to set out how the organization wishes employees to deal with e-mails, their content, style of writing and other related matters. This also applies to the use of the internet, if applicable.

The guidelines provided in the policy should not be too broad in nature, otherwise the employer may find it difficult to enforce the policy. Although the following case was decided in France, nevertheless it is probable that a judge in England and Wales may well reach a similar conclusion to that noted below.

Escota v Breil and Lucent Technologies

This case is discussed in Electronic Business Law September 2003 Volume 5 Number 8 page 16 and decided on 11 June 2003 before the Tribunal de Grande Instance de Marseille

Facts

Lucent Technologies employed Mr Nicolas Breil. He disliked Escota, a roads authority in southern France, and set up a parody web site named Escroca (the word is a play on 'escroca', which means swindles), using equipment belonging to his employer at his place of work. He featured a re-mastered version of the Escota logo, and the site included graphics of an explicit sexual nature, reinforced by further offensive materials.

Escota took legal action against:

- Mr Breil on the basis that the reproduction of the imitation of its mark and the similarity of the layout of the web site constituted an infringement of its intellectual property rights, and the views he expressed on the web site were of an abusive nature.

- Lucent Technologies, on the basis that Mr Breil created the web site whilst at work and he used his employer's equipment. Escota claimed Lucent failed to exercise proper control over the activities of its employees.

- Multimania (now Lycos), the internet service provider, which hosted the web site for failing to monitor the data stored on the site.

Decision

The members of the tribunal reached the following decisions:

- The action against Mr Breil was successful, and he was ordered to pay one Euro in damages for the infringement of Escota's intellectual property rights.

- The action against Lucent Technologies was also successful. The members of the tribunal had to assess whether the creation of the web site came within the activities for which he was employed, notwithstanding his actions were not authorized by Lucent. In reaching its conclusion that Lucent was liable, it considered the internal policy of the company, which provided that employees were allowed to visit web sites not directly related to their work, provided they did so out of working hours and did not visit illegal web sites. It was decided by the tribunal that the free use of the internet and the ability to visit any web site by employees was authorized by Lucent. Bearing in mind the lack of anything to the contrary in Mr Breil's terms of employment, the production of web sites and provision of information on personal pages could not be interpreted as being outside the limits of his job. Lucent Technologies were held jointly liable with Mr Breil. They were jointly ordered to pay the cost of advertising the decision in the case in the national newspapers.

- The action against Multimania failed, because internet service providers cannot be held liable in respect of content created by users of its service. In this instance, Multimania had taken all reasonable steps to identify the author of the web site and suspended the site immediately it was requested to do so.

Issues to cover in the policy

Ideally, the policy should be informative as well as providing rules to employees. The following list is a guideline:

- Provide an explanation of what networked communications include; an outline of the risks faced by the employer and regulations to minimise the risks whilst using the communications system effectively.

- The guidelines should state how a breach could have fatal and expensive consequences to the IT system, for instance. Employees also need to know what to expect if they are in breach of the guidelines. There is a requirement to set out what the limits are, and the employee also needs to know the boundaries that are set out by the organization.

- It has to be decided whether to permit employees to use the business communication system to send out private communications. Employees should understand that all forms of message that are sent on the organization's system are the property of the organization. The policy should make this clear, especially if it is decided to monitor communications.

- Employees should be made aware that all forms of communication, including e-mail, will be opened when they are absent from work for whatever reason, to ensure the organization is able to conduct its business in their absence.

Security

- Beware breach of confidentiality when using networked communications, in particular with the use of e-mail. Consider how much information to transfer by e-mail, including information from databases, personnel records or information received under a duty of professional confidence.

- Record all incoming and outgoing e-mails in such a way that permits demonstration of authenticity.

- Ensure the technology you use shows original unalterable copies of e-mails and provides an audit trail whenever users go back to consult the original e-mail.

- If it is impractical to store all e-mails electronically (although the low cost of storage makes this unlikely), print them off with full header information and get them signed by the member of staff dealing with the matter, although by doing this you will lose other information.

HE'S PARANOID . HE ENCRYPTS EVERY E-MAIL HE SENDS WHEN MAKING ARRANGEMENTS FOR THE ANNUAL TIDDLEYWINKS TOURNAMENT.

- It is very easy to create printed e-mails that were never sent or received.

- Sensitive material should be encrypted or sent by post. Adopt an appropriate technological solution if it is essential to prove authenticity of e-mail in certain circumstances.

Obscenity and indecency

It is important for employees to understand that if they are found to have received, downloaded or distributed obscene or indecent material over the corporate network, they are liable to both internal disciplinary proceedings and the possibility of a criminal investigation by the police. It is for this reason that employees should be made more fully aware of the risks they face if they chose to use the corporate system for this purpose.

Evidence and keeping records

Organizations have a legal duty to retain and store documents. Ensure the same occurs with all forms of networked communications used in the organization.

Retention periods

Employees must be made aware of the length of time communications are retained. They should not be misled into believing that e-mails, for instance, are deleted when they are not, and vice versa.

Time wasting

The policy should consider use of the internet for downloading games and sending jokes, and the use of instant messaging for entering virtual real-time discussions. Apart from the wasted time and the use of computer space such activities take up during the course of the day, it is possible to be put into an embarrassing position if a member of staff makes a complaint about such activities or the game is being used without a licence from the copyright owner.

Formation of contracts

It is easy for an employee to enter or amend contracts by an exchange of e-mails with the employee of another organization. Procedures should be in place to extend any authority to enter into contracts to include all forms of media.

Confidential information and trade secrets

Employees should be reminded of their duties relating to confidential information belonging to the organization and to third parties. Also, employees should be made aware that the internet is not a secure medium and that sensitive documents should not be sent over the internet without authority.

The risks that business data can be easily lost is considered so significant, that Royal & Sun Alliance announced the *removal of all cover* for damage relating to such losses for business related policies with effect from April 2002 (*UK Commercial Broker Bulletin*, Issue 04A/02) – this means that when most organizations renew their insurance policy, they will have to reconsider their system security arrangements and the effectiveness of the measures in place to prevent employees from sending out sensitive and confidential information.

Intellectual property rights

Copyright can be infringed if complete files are downloaded from the internet and if e-mails incorporate copied text. The *Copyright, Designs and Patents Act 1988* provide for civil and criminal remedies when copyright has been infringed. Downloading files from the internet or copying text into an e-mail can breach copyright, especially computer games, music files, video files or other executable material.

A number of software companies take action against companies when they can prove an infringement of copyright. In addition, the Business Software Alliance takes an active role in monitoring breaches of copyright and initiates action where they uncover evidence of transgressions by companies.

Malicious code

Consider the risk of viruses through the use of unauthorized software. Also, if a virus is exported to others, the organization could be liable in negligence for any damage caused. Consider designing a system to put e-mail attachments through a virus scanner before opening them.

On related matters, think about the system memory taken up, the lost time and cost of junk e-mail circulating within the company, such as jokes, animated cartoons, games and electronic postcards. Productive time is lost and, if such material is sent to the outside world, may cause legal action to be taken. If employees download such material, they may introduce a virus.

Defamation

E-mails in particular permit information to be sent to the outside world very easily. Employees must be made aware that e-mails are not lost forever when they are deleted and should be prohibited from transmitting, copying or forwarding material that is defamatory.

The content of networked communications

It is important to ensure that the general content of communications is carefully considered. Ill-thought out remarks expose the organization and the employee to even greater pressures if they are made in an e-mail, for instance.

> This is a message with which Jo Moore, special adviser to the Transport Secretary Stephen Byers, will probably concur, after she wrote "It's now a very good day to get out anything we want to bury" in an e-mail sent on 11 September 2001.

Harassment

Failure to deal with the issue of any form of harassment, as set out in the *Criminal Justice and Public Order Act 1994* and the *Protection from Harassment Act 1997*, can be very expensive in terms of any action an employee may take, including the legal costs, the size of damages and the loss of reputation. The Acts covers all forms of harassment, regardless of a person's race.

Communications for private use

Where the organization permits employees to use e-mail for private use, further matters must be incorporated into the relevant policy. Personal use of the e-mail, instant messaging and internet facilities can be organised along different sets of criteria, all of which have their advantages and disadvantages. The organization can allow employees to use e-mail, instant messaging and the internet with a variety of restrictions:

- Personal use being banned during working hours, but is acceptable during lunch.

- Personal use at any time, subject to guidelines.

- Unlimited personal use at any time.

Regardless of which approach is taken, the policy should ensure that guidelines are set out clearly by the organization. Issues to address include, but are not limited to:

- Pointing out that the organization owns the system and it is primarily provided for the purpose of work.

- Private use of e-mail, instant messaging and internet is acceptable providing it is reasonable and it does not contravene any of the relevant policies and guidelines, especially with regard to attachments.

It might be useful to set a limit on the amount of time an employee may spend in sending and replying to e-mails, instant messages and looking at the internet, although if parameters are set, they must be seen to be enforced to be effective. The organization will need to set out what it considers to be reasonable use. This could include such issues as not obtaining access to communication network for personal gain; the employee does not undertake any activity that is detrimental to the organization's public image and use does not interfere with work. The Information Commissioner has stated that employees must be told about the way in which private e-mails are dealt with on the system, including how long they are retained by the organization and when they are deleted.

Training

Every organization should provide sufficient and adequate training to all employees and officers in all these areas. The training should aim to:

- Create awareness of the issues to all members of staff, making them aware that their job may be in jeopardy if any action they take is detrimental to the organization.

- Explain the rationale behind the policy, and the risks that individual employees face if criminal charges are laid against them.

- Set out what standards of behaviour are expected and the types of information employees can and cannot transmit.

- Set out what the organizations policy is in relation to monitoring of e-mail and internet use.

The organization should ensure that employees are aware of the policy and the sanctions that may be imposed for not abiding by the policy. Failure to ensure employees have read and understand the policy could mean the organization fails to defend an action for unfair dismissal, as in the case of *Sangster* v *Lehman Brothers Limited* and *Carlucci* v *Oracle Corporation UK Limited*, discussed elsewhere in this text.

Tips

- Consider taking out insurance against liability for business disruption if defamatory material is inadvertently published.

- Ensure that employees know that their rights of access to computer systems must be given up on termination of employment or garden leave.

- Passwords must be changed regularly.

- Consider incorporating either confidentiality clauses or general disclaimers in company e-mails.

Applying the policy

It is crucial to ensure the policy is applied equally with each employee. Failure to apply the policy uniformly may open an organization to legitimate attacks by employees in cases where, for instance, an employer deals with one set of employees (say women) differently to another set of employees (men).

Where an employee discloses another employee's wrongdoing

Where an employee makes a protected disclosure during the course of their employment, they are protected in law against being dismissed or being treated detrimentally under the provisions of the *Public Interest Disclosure Act 1998*. The aim of the Act is to encourage and promote a culture of openness in an organization, which in turn seeks to prevent misconduct. Both employees, individuals who provide services through their own service company and agency workers are covered by the Act.

The types of disclosure that are covered by the Act are:

•   Where a criminal offence has been, is being or is likely to be committed.

•   If a person fails to comply with any legal obligation.

- Should a miscarriage of justice happen, is taking place or is likely to come about.

- Where there is evidence that the health and safety of an individual has been, is being, or is likely to be put in danger.

- Damage to the environment.

- There is a likelihood that there is a deliberate concealment of information relating to any of the above examples.

The person seeking to make a disclosure under the Act must do so in accordance with the rules, and must have a reasonable belief that the evidence upon which they intend to make the disclosure is true. One example that illustrates how this Act can be used is in the following case.

Mr P Chattenton v City of Sunderland City Council

Reference for this case: Newcastle upon Tyne employment tribunal (14 June 2000, Case No 6402938/99)

Facts

Mr Chattenton worked as a quality advisor for the City of Sunderland Council from February 1996. He shared a room with a colleague. In August 1999, he discovered pornographic images on his colleague's computer and he subsequently reported the matter to a senior manager. His colleague was subsequently suspended from work.

An internal investigation discovered that an unauthorized connection had been made to an external telephone line in another office. It was suggested that Mr Chattenton had provided some software to enable the connection to be made, which in turn permitted users to obtain access to the internet. No disciplinary action was taken against Mr Chattenton in this instance.

Mr Chattenton returned from a holiday on 27 September to discover he had been moved to an open plan office and had been given different work. He considered that these changes were to his detriment and brought a complaint to an employment tribunal. He alleged that he had been moved because he had made a protected disclosure under the terms of the *Public Interest Disclosure Act 1998*.

The City of Sunderland Council said the move from private offices to open plan was for specific reasons. They did not want such an incident to occur again, and took action to prevent employees from obtaining access to the internet inappropriately by placing all staff in the open plan office. This applied to all employees equally. In addition, he had been asked to undertake different work before he went on holiday, and before he became aware of the pornography on the computer.

Decision

The members of the tribunal decided that Mr Chattenton genuinely and reasonably believed that the pornography he discovered on the computer constituted a criminal offence. Further, it was also decided that although the pornography on the computer may not have constituted a criminal offence, this was irrelevant. It was because Mr Chattenton reasonably believed a criminal offence had been committed and he reported it to his employer. As a result, his disclosure was a protected disclosure under the terms of the Act.

It was also found that Mr Chattenton had not been treated detrimentally by being moved to an open plan office and allocated different work. It was reasonable for the employer, following this particular incident, to make the decision to accommodate all members of staff except managers in an open plan office, and just as reasonable for Mr Chattenton's manager to require him to perform the work that he had been allocated following the move.

Implications for the communications policy

Employers should have suitable procedures in place to deal with complaints from employees and contractors, should employees wish to make complaints of this nature. In particular, it is important to have a separate procedure from the normal grievance procedure, because such disclosures will invariably be made by one employee against another. Failure to deal with this issue adequately or at all will inevitably lead to legal problems and employee restlessness.

Linking policy to discipline

Failure to link the policy with the disciplinary code can be fatal. The case below illustrates that an employer needs to ensure the employee is aware that both the disciplinary procedure and the sanction reflects the seriousness of the offence. Failure to ensure both match the employee's expectations can make it more expensive in dismissing an employee.

Mr R M A Dunn v IBM United Kingdom Limited

Reference for this case: London (South) employment tribunal (1 July 1998, Case No 230587/97)

Facts

Mr Dunn was employed by IBM from 4 September 1968 until he was dismissed on 15 August 1997. On 13 August 1997 he was challenged for using his employer's equipment to obtain access to pornographic and financial web sites on the internet. He later admitted responsibility for causing offensive photographic prints to be found by an employee in a print room. It was decided that his actions constituted gross misconduct. A disciplinary meeting was convened, at which, after a brief interview, he was summarily dismissed.

Decision

Mr Dunn's complaint of unfair dismissal was upheld. The members of the tribunal did not accept that this was an instance where the Company Policy or the Business Code

---

clearly stipulated that such behaviour would automatically warrant summary dismissal. Further, in admitting the offence, Mr Dunn did not appreciate that the matter would result in a disciplinary process that would lead to his dismissal. However, the members of the tribunal took the view that his conduct and actions contributed to his dismissal. As a result, his compensation was reduced by 50 per cent.

The case was adjourned to 17 August 1998 to discuss the financial remedy. The barrister representing Mr Dunn did not attend this hearing, and the Employment Tribunal Service does not have any record of a subsequent decision. It must be surmised, therefore, that a settlement was reached between the parties without the need for a further hearing. It is probable there was a substantial settlement because of the length of Mr Dunn's service.

The investigation

It is also important to ensure that any investigation undertaken by the organization before taking disciplinary action is fair, appropriate and objective. Do not make the same mistakes that a professional body such as the Metropolitan Police made in the investigation of Sergeant Virdi in 1998.

Mr G S Virdi v The Commissioner of Police of the Metropolis

Reference for this case: London (North) employment tribunal (July, August and December 2000, Case No 2202774/98)

Facts

Letters containing racist comments were sent through the internal mail system at Hanwell and Ealing police stations on

24 December 1997 and 19 January 1998, addressed to ethnic minority members of staff. The subsequent investigation:

- Assumed that the letters were produced on computers in Hanwell police station. The reports do not indicate whether any attempt was made to establish whether the letters were printed on the printer in Hanwell police station.

- The initial investigation of the computer at Hanwell police station was carried out in such a way as to destroy evidence.

- Consideration does not seem to have been given to the possibility that relevant computer files on the system at Hanwell police station could have been transferred to floppy disks and used on another computer.

- It does not appear that any attempt was made to establish the reason why an ethnic minority Police Sergeant would want to send racist hate mail to himself and other ethnic employees.

Decision

In this instance, the Metropolitan Police were required to pay Mr Virdi a total of £151,688 by order of an employment tribunal because he was subject of discrimination because of his race. At least the Metropolitan Police could use money raised by the taxpayer to pay this sum. A business will have to raise the money by reducing the profit.

Should it be necessary to consider dismissal of an employee, the reason the employee was dismissed must be seen to be legitimate, and the dismissal was fair and reasonable. Employers will also be required to adhere to the standard dismissal and disciplinary procedure that has been introduced as a result of the *Employment Act 2002*.

Failure to investigate properly can be fatal

Whilst the ACAS "Code of Practice on Disciplinary and Grievance Procedures" is not legally binding on an organization, the Code is admissible in evidence before an employment tribunal, because it was issued under section 199 of the *Trades Union and Labour Relations (Consolidation) Act 1992*. Where members of the tribunal consider the content of the Code is relevant to any question that arises in the proceedings, they can take into account the principles contained in the Code

in relation to the disciplinary rules and procedure. As a result, employers should make themselves aware of, and act upon, the content of this Code.

Although we tend to think the police would get procedures right, the importance to the employer of making sure the investigation procedure is fair and proportionate can be crucial to the result of an action before an employment tribunal, as the following case also illustrates.

Mr B Sangster v Lehman Brothers Limited

Reference for this case: London Central employment tribunal (October 2002, Case No 2201857/2002)

Facts

Mr Sangster was employed by Lehman Brothers Limited as executive chef from 22 March 1993 to 11 January 2002. He was highly regarded as a chef by both his employer and more widely. Lehman Brothers Limited is a global investment bank, with its head office in New York, USA. Of a workforce of 13,000 employees, 3,000 work in London. There are 35 employees in the human resources department in London, and 100 in New York.

On 18 December 2001, Ms Kyle Maldiner, the human resources director in New York, received a complaint that Mr Sangster sent an offensive e-mail with attachments to an employee in Tokyo. The e-mail complained of was entitled "Mission Impossible" and had three attachments, comprising photographs of extremely obese women engaged in sexual activity with men. This e-mail had been sent to Mr Sangster, and then forwarded by him to a "Docmaster" Account and then on to the destination address, and to three fellow chefs at external e-mail addresses.

Investigation and disciplinary procedure

An investigation ensued, and Mr Sangster had a short meeting with Ms Jocelyn Battersby, human resources director for corporate areas, about this on 20 December 2001. Mr Sangster was shown the e-mail, but not the attachments. He was not suspended from working.

On 21 December 2001, Ms Carrie Osborne, executive director for human resources, reported what had occurred to Ms Maldiner in New York. Ms Osborne also indicated that the London office preferred to issue a final warning to Mr Sangster because he was a highly valued employee. Mr Maldiner disagreed, pointing out:

- The existence of the firm's use of technology policy, and, since the inception of the policy, the firm's position that people that send pornographic images will have their employment terminated.

- Reminding Ms Osborne that the employment of a managing director of the firm was terminated after 21 years' service for sending a similar image by e-mail in the past.

On 2 January 2002, Mr Gardener, the manager of executive dining, sent a letter to Mr Sangster requiring him to attend a disciplinary investigation meeting on 7 January. Mr Sangster was invited to attend this meeting with a peer as a witness.

Those present at the meeting were Mr Sangster, Mr Gardener, Ms Osborne and Ms Battersby. Mr Sangster attended this meeting without a witness, because he occupied a unique post and did not have anybody to attend with him at an equivalent level. The meeting was not adjourned to allow Mr Sangster to have a colleague present. At this meeting, Mr Sangster, who had by this time read the firm's use of technology policy, submitted a written statement in which:

- He apologised for his behaviour.

- Stated it was not his intention to cause embarrassment to anyone or bring the good name of the firm into disrepute.

- Promised that, given the opportunity, he would not let this happen again.

At no time during this interview was he informed that he might be dismissed. Mr Sangster was shown the e-mails, but was not shown the images attached to them. No attempt was made by Mr Gardener to check with Mr Sangster:

- Whether he in fact sent the e-mails.

- To whom they were sent.

- In what circumstances he sent them.

The human resources staff subsequently made recommendations to Mr Nigel Glaister, chief administrative officer of Lehman Brothers, Europe. Apparently, Mr Glaister intended to give Mr Sangster a final warning, but after he had been shown further material (Ikea and citrus fruit images), he apparently changed his view. However, the authorities in New York were adamant that Mr Sangster should be dismissed, in accordance with the global policy.

Mr Sangster was subsequently asked to attend a disciplinary meeting on 11 January 2002. At this meeting, Ms Battersby read out a statement of dismissal. Mr Sangster was not given any further opportunity to put his case, and the additional e-mails that had been found were neither considered nor shown to him at this meeting.

Mr Sangster appealed against the decision to dismiss him. Mr William Jutsum, human resources director for Europe and Mr Sherratt, a lawyer, heard the appeal. Mr Sangster attended with a witness, Mr Marley. This hearing was approached from the point of view that as Mr Sangster had admitted his misconduct, the question was whether dismissal was an appropriate response. The appeal failed. No reasons were given for the decision.

Decision and appeal

The employment tribunal held, after a hearing on 15, 16 and 17 October 2002 and 30 October 2002 in Chambers, that because of the fundamental flaws in the disciplinary process, the dismissal was procedurally unfair, and his claim for wrongful dismissal succeeded.

However, the members of the tribunal concluded that Mr Sangster contributed to his dismissal, in that his conduct was culpable and blameworthy. He sent out images that could be construed as offensive to friends, using the equipment and time of his employer. The members of the tribunal considered that his commonsense should have warned him that what he was doing was not acceptable. Whilst it was in his favour that Lehman Brothers operated their policy with double standards, nevertheless he contributed to the position he found himself in by 50 per cent.

It was held that the compensatory award would be reduced to 25 per cent of the full value, and the basic award reduced to 50 per cent of the full value. At a hearing on 17 January 2003, the members of the employment tribunal awarded the following amounts to Mr Sangster: breach of contract for wrongful dismissal £16,200, basic award (at 50 per cent) £1,500 and loss of earnings, statutory rights and future losses £27,348.

Flaws in the disciplinary process

There were substantial flaws in the way Lehman Brothers conducted the disciplinary process:

- At the investigation stage, not all the e-mails were shown to Mr Sangster, and none of the images were shown to him.

- Mr Sangster was not given the opportunity to provide a statement and he was not shown all the appropriate documentation relating to the case against him.

- Mr Sangster was asked to attend a "disciplinary investigation meeting" on 7 January. However, this was, in effect, a disciplinary hearing, after which a decision would be taken whether he should be dismissed. Had he been informed this was the case, he may have responded more carefully and in more depth than he did.

- Lehman Brothers should have adjourned the hearing for Mr Sangster to find a colleague to attend with him.

- The decision to dismiss Mr Sangster was taken by Mr Glaister, who never saw him, never spoke to him, or heard what he might have to say in mitigation.

- The actual decision to dismiss Mr Sangster was made in New York. This was not done openly, and Mr Sangster was not given the opportunity to put his case forward to those people in New York that made the decision. Also, nobody in New York took the trouble to acquaint themselves of his side of the case or take into account the individual circumstances of the case before making the decision. The decision was taken on policy grounds only, which in turn were applied inconsistently.

- The appeal hearing was a review, and therefore was not capable of curing any defect in the initial investigation process. The appeal merely endorsed the earlier decision, conducted, as it was, by manager's junior and lacking sufficient independence to those who made the original decision.

Analysis and lessons to be learnt

For a company employing 135 members of staff in the human resource offices in New York and London, it appears that Lehman Brothers made a number of errors that could have been avoided in the case of Mr Sangster. The members of the tribunal in reaching their decision in this case cited the following factors.

The use of technology policy

- It was determined that Mr Sangster did not have any or sufficient knowledge of the policy to realise what he did was regarded as gross misconduct.

- The policy was not provided to employees in hard format, but as an e-mail, to the e-mail address of each employee. It was first distributed in June 1998, and on a second occasion in June 2000. Lehman Brothers failed to determine whether Mr Sangster knew of the policy, whether he had received and read it, or if he understood the effect of the policy. If this was the only training provided to employees in relation to this matter, it cannot be considered to have been effective or appropriate. This is particularly important, given that Mr Sangster was not experienced in using a computer, and it was only in the latter months of 2001 that he became aware of how to send e-mails. Further, it appears that Ms Maldiner assumed that Mr Sangster had knowledge of the policy. Ms Osborne never contradicted this assumption.

- It was not clear from reading the policy what level of sanction would be imposed in any given case. Apparently, the New York office operated a "no tolerance" policy in respect of inappropriate content. This policy was not communicated to employees, and Mr Sangster was not made aware of it.

Other factors

The members of the tribunal, to illustrate why they reached their decision, referred to two further factors.

- An employee whose duty it was to audit e-mails passing through the system indicated that he checked proxy logs other than the one used by Mr Sangster. He knew there were, on average, between four and five people each week that obtained access to the internet and obtained much more explicit material than the images forwarded by Mr Sangster.

- The evidence submitted before the tribunal included details of two incidents that occurred in 1993 (Mr Sangster's 40th birthday) and 1997 (when a member of kitchen staff was leaving), when Mr Gardener, the manager of executive dining and Mr Sangster's line manager, invited strippers into the kitchen, during which inappropriate activity took place.

No disciplinary was taken in the case of the incidents with the strippers. In addition, it also appears that no disciplinary action was taken against the four to five individuals that downloaded more explicit material from the internet than that forwarded by Mr Sangster (it is not clear whether such material was downloaded by the same individuals each week, or if various employees within the bank were identified as downloading such materials each week).

The members of the tribunal accepted that the sending of material of the kind forwarded by Mr Sangster from Lehman Brothers clearly demonstrated gross misconduct. It was also accepted that an appropriate sanction in such circumstances could be dismissal. However, Lehman Brothers were not entitled to dismiss Mr Sangster in the circumstances of this case.

It is clear, given the facts of this case, that the procedures adopted by Lehman Brothers were not as procedurally fair as they could have been. However, it should be noted that Lehman Brothers are reported to be considering an appeal.

Equality of treatment is essential

When conducting an investigation and undertaking the disciplinary procedure, it is essential to treat all employees equally. It is also necessary to ensure the process accords with natural justice, in that managers that are responsible for taking disciplinary action should not be implicated in the actions that are the subject of the action. As will be observed in the case below, Hewlett Packard, upon taking over Compaq Computers, failed to follow good practice.

Mr R Reid, Mrs L Rankin and Mr B Graham v Compaq Computers Manufacturing Limited

Reference for this case: Employment Tribunals (Scotland) Glasgow (August and September 2003 Case No S/103021/02, S/103022/02 and S/103023/03)

Facts

Mr Reid, Mrs Rankin and Mr Graham were employed by Compaq Computers, which merged with Hewlett Packard shortly before the events giving rise to the hearing before the Employment Tribunal. During June 2002, it came to the notice of the senior management of Compaq Computers as the result of an investigation, that a number of employees and contractors were sending and receiving e-mails that contained or had images attached that contained content of a sexual nature. The investigation was conducted over a period of two to three days, during which time approximately 100 people were discovered to have breached the e-mail and internet use policy. The three applicants in this case were among those identified in the investigation. The investigation ceased because it was time consuming and disrupted normal business activities. Not every employee or contractor was investigated at the premises at Inchinnan in Renfrewshire.

Investigation and disciplinary procedure

Compaq Computers decided to hold a number of disciplinary hearings in relation to a number of the employees. The hearings were conducted by a number of managers, each of whom chaired a hearing in respect of those employees allocated to them. Prior to the hearings, a meeting was held with personnel from the human resources department, at which the criteria to be applied in determining the circumstances in which the relevant employees might face dismissal was discussed. The criteria was not clearly defined, although it was agreed that the mere receipt of e-mail, which the employee had no control over, was less serious than the transmission of an e-mail containing offensive content.

A "Mail Abuse Report" was prepared for each of the applicants. This report set out the e-mails that were sent and received, the identity of the person that sent the e-mail and the identity of the person that read the e-mail. Where an employee deleted the offending e-mails, attempts were made to trace the offending e-mail on the computer of the recipient.

An experienced person from personnel was present at each of the disciplinary hearings. Each applicant was dismissed, and their appeal against dismissal was subsequently rejected. One of the managers chairing the various disciplinary hearings was Robert Wilson, who was also Mr Graham's manager. Mr Wilson had a duty to enforce the policy that e-mails containing a sexual content were not to be disseminated by employees. Mr Graham's "Mail Abuse Report" clearly indicated that he had received an e-mail containing sexual content from Mr Wilson. It seems that Mr Wilson actively participated in the misconduct that Compaq Computers intended to eliminate. Mr Wilson's conduct was never properly investigated. One or more of the managers who had presided at the disciplinary hearings specifically brought Mr Wilson's conduct to the attention of the personnel from the human resources department. Both David Rainey, who conducted Mr Graham's disciplinary hearing, and Jan Nardini knew of the transmission of the offending e-mail by Mr Wilson. The manager and the person that heard Mr Graham's appeal also knew this fact from human resources.

Decision

The members of the tribunal drew the inference that Compaq Computers set out, quite deliberately, not to investigate Mr Wilson's conduct. Mr Wilson sent the e-mail to five people on the distribution list, and although only Mr Graham failed to delete the e-mail from his computer, the inference was that the e-mail must also have gone to the others on the list.

The members of the tribunal commented on the actions of the claimants, and point out that they knew that their conduct was inappropriate; they were responsible adults that constituted a cabal of persons who shared a taste for the kind of material that was transmitted and that the circumstances of transmission suggest it was carried out furtively. However, it was their view that the conduct of Mr Wilson was far worse than that of the claimants. This was because he was a manager and he had a duty to enforce the policy.

It was decided that the claimants were unfairly dismissed. No reduction of compensation was made, because Compaq Computers was a large undertaking which possessed an experienced and skilled human resources department, and it made a conscious decision not to investigate or discipline Mr Wilson. This decision was made, because the probable consequence was the dismissal of Mr Wilson, or, if he was not dismissed, the company could not dismiss the claimants. Further, it was also determined that the applicants did not contribute to their dismissal, because the refusal to dismiss Mr Wilson leads to the conclusion that the dismissal of the claimants was not caused or attributed to their conduct.

Each claimant was entitled to the basic award and a payment of £200 each in respect of loss of protection of employment rights. The loss suffered by Mr Reid (aged 32 with 14 years service) and Mr Graham (aged 38 with 5 years service) was quantified to cover the period of one year from the date of dismissal. In the case of Mrs Rankin (aged 27 with 6 years service) the loss suffered was quantified to cover the period of nine months from the date of dismissal. The parties were invited to work out the precise amounts between them, failing which they could apply to the tribunal to resolve the matter at a later date.

The investigation and disciplinary hearings must be impartial

In this instance, the members of the tribunal reached the conclusion that the failure to investigate Mr Wilson was deliberate. This case demonstrates that experienced members of the human resources department can fail in their duty to the organization. The lessons to be learnt from this case are:

- An investigation must be fair to everybody.

- All individuals, whatever their position, should be fully investigated where there are good reasons.

- Failure to provide training and to take effective steps to prevent widespread abuse

The members of the tribunal that heard the case of *Bower* v *Schroder Securities Limited* set out a number of factors in relation to Mr Crawshaw and his behaviour that reflected upon the lack of training provided by his employers. The following issues were included in the list:

- Mr Crawshaw was ignorant of equal opportunity matters.

- He lacked equal opportunity training.

- He did not engage in any kind of equal opportunities monitoring in respect of the bonuses awarded, on the basis of his proposals, to his analysts.

- Neither he nor his employer generally adhered to the Codes of Practice in respect of the avoidance of sex discrimination and the awarding of equal pay.

This failure to provide adequate and relevant training and support is reflected in many decisions before the employment tribunals. In the context of e-mail misuse, a recent example is that of Bob Clarke, a former sales manager for TXU Energi. The report of this case is also instructive, because it shows that attempts by TXU Energi to discourage misuse of the company e-mail system were ineffective.

Mr R V Clarke v TXU Energi

Reference for this case: Bury St Edmunds employment tribunal (October 2002 and January 2003, Case No 1501756/02)

Facts

Mr Clarke was employed as a National Sales Manager for TXU Energi from 12 February 2001 to 27 March 2002. He received an e-mail from his son, Rikki Clark, who plays cricket for Surrey. The e-mail was entitled "Why The Arabs Hate Us" and is reported to have depicted a partly naked pretty white woman sitting next to a partly naked woman of Middle Eastern appearance. The electronic image had been manipulated to make the woman of Middle Eastern appearance look ugly and hairy. On 26 February 2002, Mr Clarke distributed this image to six of the company's regional managers with the comment that it should not be passed on to anyone who could take offence at the content.

The existence of the offending e-mail was known to Mr Clerk's line manager on 8 March 2002, but no action was taken until after a meeting of 20 March 2002 between the line manager and Mr Clarke. During the course of this meeting, his line manager assured Mr Clarke that he had a secure place within the reorganization. Mr Clarke had previously threatened to resign for reasons that related to the way his line manager treated him. Mr Clarke's line manager subsequently took the decision to dismiss him.

Decision

The members of the tribunal decided that there was a potentially fair reason to dismiss Mr Clarke, but the company failed to act reasonably, citing the following reasons:

- The line manager against whom Mr Clarke had a substantial grievance was the person who decided that Mr Clarke should be dismissed.

- Although Mr Clarke was in breach of the relevant policy, he was not aware of the policy at the time he sent the e-mail. It was considered by his line manager that Mr Clarke's ignorance of the policy did not make the dismissal inappropriate.

- Mr Clarke was informed that he had the right to appeal to an independent body, but when he sought to exercise this right, he was not permitted to do so.

- The line manager that dismissed Mr Clarke had no training in the gradations of penalty that were intended to be applied. Alternative penalties were not considered.

- It was clear that the attempts by the company to discourage the misuse of the corporate e-mail system was not effective, as indicated by the numbers of individuals that were under investigation for using the e-mail system inappropriately. This was not taken into account when deciding what penalty to apply to Mr Clarke.

It was decided that Mr Clarke's actions did not constitute a repudiatory breach of his contract, and therefore he was unfairly dismissed. However, the members of the tribunal decided that Mr Clarke demonstrated a lack of leadership and acted inappropriately in sending the potentially offensive e-mail. In so doing, his conduct contributed to his dismissal. The compensatory award was reduced by 40 per cent to take account his blameworthy conduct.

Mr Clarke was awarded: a basic award of £375, a compensatory award of £8,092.80 and damages for breach of contract for failure to give notice £24,404.

Providing adequate training to managers is essential

The case of *Clarke* above, as with the case of *Sangster* v *Lehman Brothers Limited*, illustrates how something as simple as failing to ensure basic processes and procedures relating to the disciplinary procedure are followed can expose the organization to unnecessary expense. It is necessary to understand that for an action by an employee to constitute misconduct, the organization should be aware of the factors that will help determine whether the resultant disciplinary sanction was appropriate in the circumstances. A more recent case illustrates why training is essential. In the case of *Karen Carlucci* v

Oracle Corporation UK Limited, Karen Carlucci made a number of claims, including sex discrimination and unfair dismissal. This case is discussed only in relation to the 'Boys' Club Culture'.

Karen Carlucci v Oracle Corporation UK Limited

Reference for this case: Reading employment tribunal (September 2004 to March 2004, Case No 2700870/03 and 2702150/03)

Facts relevant to the 'Boys' Club Culture'

Karen Carlucci was initially employed as an account manager in retail and services, and later became an application sales manager in communications and media, based in London. In 2002 she achieved 158 per cent of her sales quota and was ranked eight at Oracle for sales. In almost ten years of employment in sales, Karen Carlucci reached her target sales quota in six out of ten years. It was alleged by Karen Carlucci that the culture within Oracle was male orientated. Part of the evidence in relation to this claim was an e-mail circulated by Adrian Wotton, regional director of commercial and industrial sales, to his team, including Karen Carlucci, on 14 November 2002. The attachment to the e-mail began:

> "We always hear the 'Rules' from a female's side now there are the rules from a male's side. There are our Rules! Please note …. These are numbered '1' ON PURPOSE!"

The members of the tribunal in their decision noted a number of the rules:

> "Learn to wipe the toilet seat. You are a big girl. If it's up put it down. We need it up, you need it down. You don't hear us bitching about you leaving it down.

> Come to us with a problem only if you want to help solving it. That's what we do. Sympathy is what your girlfriends are for.

Let us ogle. We are going to look anyway: it's genetic.

Don't ask us what we are thinking about unless you are prepared to discuss such topics as farting, beer, the 4-4-2 formation and cars."

Mr Wotton was asked in cross-examination whether he considered it an appropriate e-mail to circulate. He replied "In the context this was sent yes – in other contexts no."

The members of the tribunal offered the following comments:

"87 Mr Wotton's evidence highlighted was his attitude and the male orientated culture in which the applicant worked. He simply gave no thought as to whether or not such an email was appropriate for circulation within an office environment. Of the addressees to whom the rules were circulated within the respondent only 2 were female out of a total of 10 addressees. The Tribunal consider Mr Wotton's attitude to that email and his actions in circulating it as clear evidence of a culture within the respondent that quite simply did not take proper account of the need to guard against stereotypical gender assumptions in dealing with female staff to ensure equal treatment of both women and men."

Decision

The members of the tribunal found that Karen Carlucci suffered from sex discrimination and victimisation, and was awarded £95,032.11, comprising £69,644,35 loss of earnings; £2,816.70 interest; injury to feelings £15,000 and interest of £2,570.96. It was also determined that she was unfairly dismissed and received a basic award of £1,820 and a compensatory award of £1,354. The reader should note that this was a more complex case that the description of the culture as described above.

This case demonstrates the need to ensure proper training is given to all members of staff in relation to all aspects of life within an organization, and any failure to treat such matters seriously can lead to unpleasant results for everybody concerned, including the organization. In this case, the members of the tribunal noted, in paragraph 19 of the decision, that '... there is no practical framework in place at the respondent company through which to implement the principle of equal opportunities. The code of ethics is itself a general expression of principle. The Tribunal find it extremely surprising that given the size of the respondent's organisation no written practical framework currently exists to assist in the active operation on a daily basis of an Equal Opportunities policy.'

The members of the tribunal continued:

'20 The Tribunal take into account the lamentable lack of training of any of the applicant's Line Managers in equal opportunities policies. The respondent appears content to focus training activities in terms of seminars and courses on those activities that maximise the respondent's sales successes and revenue generation. Such training as there is in equal opportunities is on a "self service" modular basis through e-training. When examined in evidence by the Tribunal that training appeared to relate to business ethics. There was no specific evidence before the Tribunal of any implementation of and monitoring of equal opportunities in order to supply information to the respondent's management.'

Tips

- An employer must undertake a fair and reasonable investigation into an alleged breach of the disciplinary code before taking any action against the employee.

- Where an organization has an e-mail and internet acceptable use policy, there should be evidence that all employees received it, were made aware of it, understand the effect of the policy, are aware of the sanctions and receive proper training.

- Appropriate disciplinary procedures should be in place. They should be fair and reasonable and include the right for an employee to be accompanied at interviews and permit an appeal against any disciplinary decision made.

- Appropriate training should be given to those members of staff with the authority to exercise functions within the terms of the disciplinary code.

- The conduct under question should be assessed against other types of e-mail and internet misuse, and any penalty imposed should take into account how others have been dealt with. Where an employee has used the corporate system for unlawful activities, the penalties can be more severe.

- Mitigating factors should be considered, such as the explanation offered by the employee; length of service, job and level of seniority; how long they have been employed and their record whilst in employment.

CHAPTER 9
OPERATIONAL IMPLEMENTATION
OF THE POLICY

> **Writing the network communications use policy is only the first step**

Having developed an acceptable network communications use policy, an organization may consider it has gone some way to satisfy one corporate governance topic. However, developing and implementing a policy is only part of the equation. The wider picture is outlined in more detail below, illustrating the considerations that must be taken into account before the organization can truly show it has covered the use and misuse of networked communications properly and comprehensively. Some questions are pertinent:

- How do members of staff use the policy?

- How does the organization know the policy is not abused?

- What effect does the policy have on the behaviour of the individual employee?

- How many organizations have an e-mail system in place that ensures users and administrators cannot get around the policy and abuse the system?

Where the policy is proved not to have been implemented properly (where, for instance, an incident occurs that may also become public knowledge), the failure may also indicate an inadequate approach by the organization towards corporate governance. This, in turn, may also demonstrate a dilatory attitude towards complying with the requirements of legislation, such as the *Data Protection Act 1998*. Whether public sector or private business, senior management will increasingly be required to address these issues in the future.

The purpose of the policy

The intention behind the development and implementation of a suitable policy is two-fold: to reduce risk to both the organization and the individual employee. It protects the righteous. The aim should be to reduce the wasted time and the costs of dealing with the misuse of the corporate communication system by employees.

Undoubtedly, some employees may consider the imposition of such a policy illustrates a tendency by the employer to be over protective towards its employees, or demonstrates the inability of the employer to trust their employees to be sensible when using the communications system. Whilst it is correct to say that most employees can be trusted to use the networked communications system sensibly, nevertheless the provision of rules, guidance and linking the policy to the disciplinary code is essential if employers are to control those employees that persist in acting recklessly.

An employer usually takes time and money to recruit an employee. It is probably the case that most employers seek to ensure they select a new employee because of the skills the employee will bring to the organization. As a result, employers prefer to retain valued members of the organization. To protect the investment in employees, therefore, the employer must implement appropriate policies to ensure lapses in discipline are discovered, investigated properly and any decisions made are proportionate to the seriousness of the transgression.

Hence the need for relevant policies. Hence the need to understand there is more to a communications policy than merely writing and implementing it.

Implementing the policy

Many readers that have been instrumental in developing and e-mail and internet use policy in the past will accept that the process of implementing the policy follows, more or less, the following pattern:

- The policy is developed by setting down, discussing and improving the content. This tends to be initiated by the organization and in the interests of the organization, although members of staff may be invited to offer comments as successive drafts are prepared, reviewed and approved.

- Training is usually provided to members of staff. The type and quality of training will depend on the perceived risk, as well as the size and internal structure of the organization. Whether whatever training is provided is appropriate, sufficient or adequate, will be demonstrated by the numbers of employees that are discovered to contravene the policy.

- After the policy is developed and training given, employees enjoy a short period of awareness of the issues surrounding the use of e-mail.

Thereafter, as with other policies, the organization will review the policy and keep it up-to-date. The frequency by which this process occurs is a matter of judgment, but should not be sporadic, because new examples of abuse are reported more frequently than many employers prefer.

Whilst the implementation of the policy may be straightforward, the operation of the policy is frequently ignored. It is how the operational aspects of the communications system run that distinguish those organizations that have merely written a policy and those that understand, implement and are shown to operate the policy effectively. An organization can only state that corporate communications are 'compliant' and fully understand what this means when it can continually demonstrate that the operation of the policy is sound. The successful operation of the communications policy depends on:

- The response by individual employees.

- The implementation of the policy and how the organization can demonstrate the policy has been implemented.

The response by individual employees

Employees will benefit from high quality training in the pitfalls of using networked communications. Ideally, such training, which may be refreshed with up-dates, will ensure most employees can be trusted to implement the policy on their own.

> **If just one employee contravenes the policy, loss of reputation may well follow.**

However, where employees contravene the policy, the cost to the organization can be significant. When the policy is operating effectively, it is possible to reduce the risk of this group of employees offending, because when employees know they will get caught, they will tend not to take the risk of breaking the rules. This will benefit both the organization and the individual. Those employees that follow the policy do not build up a grievance against those employees that are known to ignore the policy, but do not get caught. The benefit to the employer is that infractions of the policy can be quickly discovered and dealt with appropriately, thus maintaining high moral amongst the staff.

To demonstrate the policy is operationally effective, it is important for the organization to show, with good quality evidence, when employees have acted properly. By being able to check the individual behaviour of each employee, good behaviour is positively reinforced. One method of getting the message over to employees that they have acted in accordance with the policy is to have a system in place that immediately identifies those few employees that refuse to act in accordance with the policy. The act of catching an employee who has broken the terms of the policy helps to reinforce the behaviour of those that follow the policy.

Finally, one employee or group of employees are particularly exposed to allegations of wrongdoing by both fellow employees and management within the organization. This is the administrator of a system, or administrators, if more than one person. The administrator is required to have access to trusted data by the very nature of the task they perform. However, where the data on a system is not audited, it may be difficult for an administrator to show they have not abused their privileged rights of access. As a result, the enforcement of the communications policy should include a fully functioning audit trail whenever an administrator obtains access to trusted data. An audit trail will, in turn, enable the good administrator to show that they have not abused their privileges.

The response by the organization

The response of the organization to the problems inherent in the use of networked communications tends to be:

- To write an appropriate policy, train members of staff and (perhaps) link it with the disciplinary procedure.

- Buy technical solutions, such as virus checking and content scanning.

Technical solutions

By themselves, technical solutions are normally not sufficient. They are important, but cannot offer a complete answer. For instance, many organizations fail to identify whether content scanning or blocking solutions actually perform correctly. Further, the richness of the English language, when taken out of context (or deliberately placed into an ambiguous context) can overcome the scanning software. In addition, words with an innocuous meaning can also be used to put over a contrary meaning that can be malicious. Whilst the rules can be changed on content scanning solutions to take account for the requirements of the organization, the software cannot be foolproof, and false positives and undetected negatives will continue to occur.

Document retention and disposal policy

Furthermore, few organizations have incorporated their networked communications system into the document retention and disposal policy. For instance, not all e-mails need to be retained for the same time, and although storage is a cost that needs to be monitored, the organization is required to retain certain communications (including e-mails and instant messages, if a regulator requires all forms of message to be retained) for set lengths of time, in accordance with relevant legislation and regulation.

The legislative burden and personal data

Also, politicians have increased the burden on organizations with legislation that requires careful attention to detail, record keeping and auditing. In particular, the fifth data protection principle of the *Data Protection Act 1998* prevents the organization from retaining personal data for longer than is necessary. If employees are permitted to use the e-mail facilities to send and receive private e-mail, how does the organization ensure it does not breach this requirement? In this respect, additional problems will begin to occur when (or if) employees start to take action under the terms of the *Human Rights Act 1998*, especially in respect to their rights of respect for private and family life and freedom of expression.

Organizations should also bear in mind that the vast majority of e-mails that pass through the system contain personal data, because the sender and recipient are identified by their name. In addition, the seventh principle of the *Data Protection Act 1998* requires the organization to secure personal data. If employees or administrators can gain access to any employee's e-mail, the organization is clearly failing in its duty in accordance with this principle.

Searching for data

Already, organizations are required to provide copies of relevant personal data in accordance with the provisions of the provisions of the *Data Protection Act 1998* to people that make subject access requests. This burden will increase now the *Freedom of Information Act 2000* is in force, because organizations in the public sector will be required to search for and provide vast quantities of information when requests are made.

In this respect, how many organizations can say that their searching facilities:

- Are effective.

- Do not breach the seventh data principle during the course of the life of an e-mail, in that nobody is permitted to read the content without authority.

- Do not expose the organization to claims that they are withholding information because it is not a complete "set" of the personal data requested. The organization needs to explain why they have not produced all the documents requested, because many e-mails may have been deleted under the terms of the relevant document retention and disposal policy.

Until recently, the business requirements of the communications system have been overlooked. An organization needs to have an effective search mechanism, so a search can be made in relation to the content of a message or the attachments to e-mail messages in particular. By having such a search feature (which in itself must be subject to an audit trail), the organization can more readily respond to requests for information under the *Data Protection Act 1998* and *Freedom of Information Act 2000*.

Richard Thomas, when he gave his first interview after taking over as Information Commissioner, told Bob Sherwood in an article published in the Financial Times on 8 January 2003, that he would not accept any excuses from any public body that was not able to handle requests for information when the *Freedom of Information Act 2000* is in force. He is quoted as saying "Two years from now is a decent length of time for public authorities to get their act together and to anticipate what requests they will be receiving so I wouldn't really see that many legitimate excuses for difficulties." It will be interesting to see what action, if any, will be taken against those organizations that fail to have effective search and retrieval facilities in place.

An audit trail can be crucial

Failing to link the policy to the disciplinary procedure is fatal. Whilst it may be rare for an individual to challenge the evidence of wrongdoing, nevertheless there will come a time when an employee or an employer will seek to demonstrate the evidence is either tainted (and therefore cannot be relied upon) or has been tampered with (and cannot therefore be used at all), thus negating the purpose of the policy.

Where an infraction of the policy has been uncovered, it is important to ensure there is probity of evidence. This is important, regardless of whether the case is heard internally. If the evidence has a clear audit trail, it is possible that it will be acceptable to a court or tribunal. As a result, the quality of the evidence may permit the organization to defend an action for unfair dismissal. Alternatively, such evidence may ensure the organization does not have to defend legal proceedings, as in the case mentioned below.

The case of *Jacques* v *Queensland Police Service* occurred in Australia, by which a policeman on probation sought to be re-instated in his post, and the police service relied upon the integrity of the audit trails of the electronic evidence to resist his reinstatement.

Glen Andrew Jacques v Queensland Police Service

Reference for this case: Queensland Industrial Relations Commission (No B325 of 1994)

Facts

In 1993 Jacques, a police constable, was the subject of a complaint in relation to sexual harassment. He was issued with a Show Cause Notice in writing on 5 January 1994, alleging that his general standard of conduct had been below that expected of a police officer, and an investigation had revealed conduct that would warrant the preferring of disciplinary charges. The notice included allegations of sexual harassment of a female officer, being untruthful when questioned about his conduct, attempting to evade the issue by making a counter allegation against the female officer and attacking fellow officers by claiming that everyone who disagreed with his version was lying or out to get him. He was subsequently dismissed from the Queensland Police Service.

He made an application to the Queensland Industrial Relations Commission in 1996 to be reinstated because he claimed he was dismissed unfairly. It was claimed that the original harassment took place over the telephone. He denied making the telephone call. As a result, the Police Service were required to check their telephone records to verify the time and date of the call, and the location of the telephone extension.

The importance of the audit trail

An analysis of the audit trail revealed that the ex-police constable had used the computer system at the time the telephone call was made. A further analysis revealed a pattern of misuse by him over a period of fourteen months, during which he had questioned his neighbours, friends, relatives and others who had previously made complaints against him. He had also carried out checks on both current and previous senior members of the service, including members who had died in the line of duty.

Although the security officer gave evidence for the Queensland Police Service, he was not cross-examined, because the application for reinstatement was withdrawn. The quality of the evidence of the audit trail enabled the telephone logs to be adduced as evidence, which helped to discredit the ex-police constable, and which also helped to corroborate the evidence of the witnesses.

This example helps to demonstrate it is important that:

- Nobody has abused the system.

- No employee or administrator has altered or deleted records.

- The administrator has not viewed the records inappropriately.

The need for quality audited evidence

From the point of view of adducing evidence in a court or an employment tribunal, there is a clear requirement for a fully audited evidential trail to show if abuse has occurred. This case illustrates that it may be necessary to demonstrate the:

- Integrity of the communications system, including e-mail and instant messaging (i.e. nobody – including an administrator – can change the contents of an e-mail without leaving an audit trail, or no employee can delete another employee's e-mail without appropriate authority).

- Authenticity of the audit trail for each e-mail, and each time the e-mail is viewed.

- Comprehensive nature of the information that should be made available, such that no elements relating to the e-mail are missing.

Guidance in relation to audit trails and how they should be dealt with are considered in detail in 'An International Code of Practice for electronic Documents and e-business Transactions' DISC PD 5000-1:2000. Organizations will need to pay careful attention to protect evidence in the future. There are a number of reasons for this:

- Assume the administrator conducts searches properly and in the course of their employment. One problem that may arise is whether they have abused their rights in conducting the search: should the administrator, for instance, have access to the content of an e-mail when searching for personal data when requested to do so under the terms of the *Data Protection Act 1998* in accordance with a request from a data subject? It is more appropriate for an administrator to conduct a less revealing search, only looking for the appearance of the name of a "data subject", a process that can be automated.

- It is very easy to cut and paste an e-mail. To provide for the integrity of each change to an e-mail, it is important to have an audited history of each change throughout its life. This means that each time an e-mail is looked at, the action is noted on the audit trail – and nobody should be able to alter the audit trail, not even the administrator.

- Finally, to prevent the administrator altering the audit trail, there should also be an audit trail to audit the administrator's actions.

Ensuring the policy is fully operational

There are a number of core issues than any organization must consider with respect to the use and abuse of the corporate communication facilities:

- How many organizations can clearly demonstrate that their policy is being implemented properly?

- What evidence is available to show that the implementation of the policy satisfies the requirements relating to corporate governance and compliance with legislation?

- How can it be demonstrated that the policy is having the desired effect in reducing risks and is adequate for the purpose?

Perhaps Dan Corry, a former special adviser to Stephen Byers at the Department of Transport, may wish his actions has been the subject of greater scrutiny. He sought to establish the political allegiance of members of the Paddington rail crash survivors' group. On 23 May 2002, he wrote an e-mail to the Labour Party, the text of which was published after the press became aware of the exchange of e-mails in June:

> "Can you get some sort of check done on the people who are making a big fuss on the Paddington Survivors group attacking SB please (i.e. the ones taking over from Pam Warren). The names are in the press."

In response to what sort of check was to be made, he replied, "Basically, they are Tories". In response to the furore that accompanied the expose of these e-mails, Mr Corry apologised unreservedly and said it was wrong of him to have sent them.

The above example, amongst the many examples set out in this text, indicate how important it is for those at the highest levels in an organization to ensure they do not encourage such a negative and aggressive culture to develop in the course of its day-to-day activities.

Putting a networked communications policy into operational effect requires more than merely writing a policy and training members of staff. Apart from the regular training of employees to the appropriate quality, and the use of appropriate technical solutions that will aid the organization in implementing the policy, more needs to be done before any organization can truly say that they have implemented the policy operationally. The problems with implementing the policy is graphically highlighted with the following case.

> ### *Helen Brearley v Timber Taylors UK Limited*
>
> **Reference for this case:** Nottingham Employment Tribunal case number 2601401/2004
>
> **Facts**
>
> Helen Brearley, a designer aged 41 of Alfreton. Ms Brearley was dismissed in March 2004 for gross misconduct by Timber Taylors, a shopfitting company in Bulwell, Nottingham, after the company read the e-mail correspondence she exchanged with her partner, Theresa Millward, aged 27. Apparently, the company monitored her e-mails, the use of the mobile telephone provided to her by the company, and her use of the internet for three months, because her use of the networked communications system was considered unreasonable and in violation of the relevant policy. The commercial manager, Chris Samples, pointed out that:
>
> - The volume of e-mails were excessive, in that 300 e-mails were sent by Ms Brearley.
>
> - The content of some 36 of them contained sexually explicit language, which Ms Brearley was fully aware of, because Miss Millward reacted to the content of on e-mail by responding: 'I'm surprised that got through our mail sweep', to which Ms Brearley replied: 'I can make them even more dirty if you like.'

- Some of the e-mails were alleged to contain profane language.

Apparently, she also used the mobile telephone to make dozens of calls to her lover. In her defence, Ms Brearley is reported to have told the members of the employment tribunal that the e-mails helped her through the day, because she struggled to cope with both personal and work-related stress. She knew her e-mails were monitored, but thought she had a reasonable degree of privacy in her correspondence.

It is reported that Stephen Keevash, the tribunal chairman, said that 'The employee had been given no prior warning that her behaviour warranted criticism, and undoubtedly if she had been she would have stopped.' The members of the tribunal determined that the company had grossly overstated the problem, and a warning would have been a more appropriate in the circumstances. Ms Brearley was awarded £26,245.87. At the time this text was prepared, the company announced it intended to appeal this decision.

This case illustrates the difficulty all organizations face when dealing with such matters. As the examples of misuse in this text illustrates, some employees assume they have a right to use the communications system, and rarely consider the consequences of their actions – either to themselves or to the organization. There is a delicate line to be drawn between implementing the policy and taking appropriate action to curb and prevent misuse. Before taking action against an employee, it is crucial to:

- Record the reasons for beginning an investigation.

- Ensure appropriate authority has been given to the investigator (whether the IT or personnel departments) to undertake an investigation, especially where an employee's communications are to be monitored.

- Where action is considered, care must be taken to ensure the reaction is proportionate to the circumstances of the case.

Whilst e-mail, instant messaging and similar forms of networked communications are considered to be a significant advantage to most organizations, nevertheless the risks attendant upon its use are manifest. Every organization will need to take particular care to ensure they demonstrably implement the operation of their policy effectively, and not just trust to luck by asking employees to police themselves.

CHAPTER 10
TECHNICAL SOLUTIONS

> **Software vendors have begun to address the problem**

A number of technical products have begun to appear on the market that will help with the storage of e-mails in particular, although the issue is wider than just e-mail communications. The buyer should be aware that the solutions on offer differ in the way the product is designed. The design of the software affects the way e-mails are stored. In addition, some products have audit trails. Whilst some products provide for pure storage, others have been designed to enable the organization to comply with legal and regulatory requirements.

Invariably, the solutions will not be suitable for every organization, and many organizations will have such complex requirements, that the comments offered in this chapter can only discuss the issues within the legal context. Clearly, additional analysis will be required for more complex infrastructures.

The journalling facility

One point should be made in relation to the facility provided by Microsoft for journalling in Exchange. When an e-mail is sent or received, a copy goes direct to the journal mailbox. The reader will be aware that the e-mails stored in this way are subject to the various legal requirements set out in this text. However, there are a number of issues that illustrate how vulnerable this facility can be. Some are IT management concerns, whilst others have legal ramifications.

Managing the problem

It is impractical to leave all the e-mail messages in the journal mailbox for the following reasons:

- The Microsoft Exchange server message store will continue to increase in size over time, which will cause the server to get progressively slower. As a corollary to the increase in data, the time taken to back up the server will also increase. The cumulative effect of progressively increasing volumes of data will, in turn, affect the time it takes the IT department to restore a system from a backup tape.

- The sheer volume of e-mails stored in the journal makes a search more difficult, especially because none of the e-mails are indexed.

- Large numbers of e-mails may be in the journal mailbox that should be stored elsewhere, such as e-mails that have to retained for long periods, as set out in the document retention and disposal policy. As the examples below demonstrates, it may not be appropriate to have every e-mail stored in the journalling mailbox that is difficult to search, too big and lacks the basic auditing requirements set out below.

The legal perspective

A significant weakness with some versions of the journalling facility is the ability of an administrator to switch the facility off or delete the entire database. Further issues include the following:

- The time and date stamp facility is not protected to prevent the time and date from being altered.

- E-mails can be viewed in clear text without leaving an evidential trail.

- A copy of the entire journal can be taken without leaving an audit trail.

As a result of these weaknesses, it is possible for a person to log into the journal mailbox, extract e-mails, alter their content and then save them back to the mailbox. Where the Microsoft Exchange server logs this activity, the person could then go to the server and delete the entire log file, thus removing any evidence of the action.

Points to consider when thinking about buying a software product

If a technical solution is to provide for a degree of certainty in relation to the issues raised in this guide, there is a need to consider some of the issues set out below. Although these points are directed towards e-mail, nevertheless the same principles apply to any other form of communication held in electronic format:

- Prevent employees from deleting, cutting and pasting e-mails at will by documenting every change to each e-mail in real time (or as near to real time as is possible) as it is sent, returned, copied and where text is cut and pasted. The aim should be to create a new record, and therefore a new e-mail, every time an e-mail is altered.

- Prevent the administrator from having access to e-mails without an audit trail of their actions being immediately apparent on an inspection of the system (this protects the administrator and the organization).

- As a corollary to the two previous points, there is a need to ensure a record is made in the audit trail every time an e-mail is recovered and opened, which in turn provides details of each person that undertakes this activity.

- Archive each relevant e-mail securely in real time (or as near to real time as possible), and to archive each change to each e-mail, thus ensuring e-mails cannot be viewed or altered without leaving an audit trail.

- Ideally, not to archive every e-mail received for the same length of time, because many e-mails may not need storing (such as private e-mails or those that contain comments that do not need to be retained for any business reason). Even if a technical solution has the ability to enable the organization to select the type of e-mails that are stored, and the length of time a particular e-mail must be stored, such a solution may not be the best answer. There is a need to delete e-mails containing personal data,

but a large majority of e-mails contain a mix of personal information and business information. It has become normal to mix social intercourse with business, or different types of business in the same e-mail. As a result, although the ideal solution is to have a technical system that can delete e-mails in accordance with set policies, the very nature of e-mail, being unstructured, mean that the introduction of such a solution may cause additional problems of retention.

- Provide an audit trail for every e-mail and every attachment, to ensure no employee can abuse the system and delete e-mails, or send pornographic attachments, or add information such as additional recipients, attachments or text by getting around the document retention and disposal policy.

- Create a policy that applies at the organizational level that prevents individuals making independent decisions about the retention and disposal of e-mails on their computer. It is for the organization at the highest level to set the appropriate retention dates. Policies are required to set out how long the e-mail will be stored for; where the e-mail will be stored (online or offline); how many copies will be retained and on what type of media. Whenever the organization decides to change a policy affecting the life cycles of a category of e-mail, it is important to ensure an audit trail is created to document the change.

- Search quickly and effectively for data to comply with requests and duties under the *Data Protection Act 1998* and *Freedom of Information Act 2000*.

- The encryption of all e-mails that are archived, which can help the organization comply with the requirements of the *Data Protection Act 1998*, and will prevent administrators from viewing the content of e-mails unless they are authorized to undertake a search.

The organization should aim to prevent individuals making independent decisions about the retention and disposal of e-mails on their computer. This is because employees do not necessarily adhere to the policy. Mr Graham Maher, in-house solicitor at British American Tobacco, gave evidence in the McCabe case on this matter. He said employees "were lax in their compliance with the records management policy, and had kept documents for longer than the policy specified".

Also, where a technical solution is considered, careful attention should be paid to the guidance offered in 'An International Code of Practice for electronic Documents and e-business Transactions' DISC PD 5000-5:2000, comprising Part 5 – Using Trusted Third Party Archives, where the solution provider stores and deals with e-mail archiving and storage on behalf of the organization.

It is possible that an appropriate solution can help to:

• Monitor how the communications system is being used.

• Index, search and retrieve e-mails that are archived, which is not an activity that is construed as interception.

• Add weight to any disclaimers included in the e-mails sent out by the organization at present. If the e-mail system does not have an audit trail for each e-mail sent and received, any disclaimer used is of little value. This is because cutting and pasting comments in an ordinary e-mail is easy.

• The ability to alter the contents of an e-mail reduces the weight to be attached to a disclaimer.

• Conduct searches more effectively and for less cost.

• It may reduce the cost of preparing for a dispute.

• Reduce the abuse of the communications system when users realise that each e-mail sent and received cannot be repudiated or challenged.

The organization needs to consider how it is going to carry out its duty to retain and dispose of networked communications in accordance with the wide variety of inconsistent legislation and regulations that deal with the retention of documents. It is possible that Norwich

Union may not have faced the problems they experienced if a suitable technical e-mail archiving and retention solution was available and in operation at the relevant time. Once each employee becomes aware that every e-mail they send and receive:

- Is retained.

- The content is subject to an audit trail.

- Every change made creates a separate, audited, new document.

- Has a retention period.

- Will be archived.

It is probable that they will be less likely to send the corporate database to their personal e-mail account or to a competitor or the press.

Internal control and corporate governance

To fulfil the corporate duty of care towards corporate governance, as outlined in 'Internal Control: Guidance for Directors on the Combined Code', published by the Institute of Chartered Accountants in 1999 (the Turnbull report, which is subject to revision), it is necessary to monitor internal control mechanisms. By including the communications system within the ambit of the Guidance, the organization will be seen to recognise a risk exists and demonstrate that it is actively monitoring the exposure all organizations face when using networked communications in the workplace.

Networked communications is a multi-disciplinary problem within the organization

Dealing with networked communications use is not the sole responsibility of the IT department. It is a matter for information technology, human resources and the data controller, as pointed out by the Information Commissioner in note 2 to chapter 1 "Managing data protection" in "The Employment Practices Data Protection Code for Employment Records". It is also a matter for the company secretary or records manager.

> The human resources departments of most organizations spend more time on disciplinary action for the misuse of e-mail than for any combination of cases involving dishonesty, violence and breaches of health and safety rules.

Employers must pay careful attention to networked communications in the workplace. Senior management and members of the board can no longer ask the IT manager or their department to deal with some of the varied issues that the use of networked communications entail. All organizations of any size will need to ensure that human resources (or the personnel department), the data controller, risk controller and IT departments are all involved with dealing with the risks that accompany the use of networked communications.

As this text indicates, the use of networked communications encompasses several issues, all of which must be taken into account by the organization:

* Whether to permit personal use or not, and if so, how to deal with personal e-mails.

* Proper training (not just writing a policy and getting every member of staff to sign to acknowledge they have received a copy of the

policy) of all staff in the risks to both the organization and to them personally, that go with using networked communications.

- Ensuring that monitoring the use of the communications infrastructure, if it takes place, is conducted correctly.

- Securing and encrypting e-mail data in accordance with the employer's duties under the terms of the *Data Protection Act 1998*.

- Establishing an appropriate networked communications use policy, putting it into operational effect, keeping it up-to-date and linking it to the disciplinary and grievance procedure.

- Ensuring communications are dealt with in accordance with the document retention and disposal policy.

- Being aware of the cost to the organization if e-mails are to be used in evidence, whether in an employment tribunal or in litigation.

Organizations must pay careful attention to their networked communications infrastructure, because the examples used in this text indicate that the problems will not go away. It is arguably better to avoid the costs of litigation and the publicity this creates. The organization should aim to reduce the risks, add to the bottom line or, if an organization funded by the taxpayer (whether local or central government, National Health Service or any other publicly funded organization), to reduce waste and not increase the burden on the taxpayer, and reduce costs.

For all organizations, whether in the public or private sector, the opening years of the twenty first century have begun to place a premium on reputation. Failing to respond to the risks adequately will mean:

- Businesses face a lost reputation and a reduction of market value.

- Professionals, should they leak confidential personal information, will invariably face heavy penalties imposed by professional bodies.

- Public bodies will suffer loss of reputation and the individuals involved in failing to deal with the issues surrounding the risk will be held responsible, with inevitable consequences.

Failure to deal with the use of networked communications at work will cause losses that can be avoided. The risks are a known quantity. Whether leadership in the organization will deal with the risk effectively is a matter of good governance. To discover whether you need to think about resolving any problems you have by buying more technology, test whether there is a gap between your perception that you have got it under control and the reality. The bigger the gap, the bigger the problem.

APPENDICES

APPENDIX 1
CHECK LIST FOR THE NETWORK
COMMUNICATIONS USE POLICY

The list below is provided as a guide to help write or revise the relevant network communications use policies. The check list does not provide an exhaustive note of everything an organization must consider, partly because every organization has different needs. Some communication infrastructures are more complex than others; confidentiality requirements will differ from one organization to another, and some will operate in several jurisdictions, thus causing other problems relating to privacy laws. It is hoped that the reader will find it to be a useful guide, in combination with the information set out in the text of the book.

The aim is to:

- Set out, in broad terms, what should be included in the policy.

- Remarks are offered that may emphasise certain issues that the reader might wish to pay particular attention to.

- Where there are examples that serve to illustrate what went wrong (or how an organization did something correctly), a reference to a case is given.

For obvious reasons, the guidance noted below is not exhaustive, but aims to cover the most relevant issues.

Formulating the policy

People that should be involved with the formulation of the policy include:

- Company secretary or the equivalent in the public sector.

- In-house lawyers.

- Human resources professionals.

- The data controller.

- Information technology staff.

- Risk analysis staff.

- Senior staff or board members.

- Where relevant, trade union representatives.

The aim should be to ensure each department is more fully aware of the particular issues that it has to deal with, and to share their concerns with others to engender active methods of preventing misuse of the organization's infrastructure.

Informative

The employer has a duty to set the standards that are acceptable within the organization. As a result, the policy should set out what it is intended to achieve, such as to explain why a policy is necessary; the potential for legal liability (with examples, if thought appropriate); to set out what conduct is acceptable and what is not acceptable, and what, if any, monitoring that takes place on the system. What should be included in the policy:

- Explanation of what forms of communications makes up the networked communications infrastructure, including what e-mail and instant messaging is, and how the internet works. The Information Commissioner has indicated that the employer must indicate to the employee how files that are downloaded from the internet are stored, where they are stored and when they are deleted. Employees must also be aware of the length of time e-mails are stored and when they are deleted.

- Consider including an outline of the legal liability faced by the employer and the employee.

- How long networked communications are stored for; where they are stored; what security provisions have been put in place to provide for the security of personal data and the policy relating to what the organization does with communications after the employee leaves the organization.

In addition, advice should be given to employees on the circulation of business related communications, especially with reference to:

- The use of "cc" and "bcc" options for the distribution of e-mail. Employees should be reminded that it is unnecessary to use these attributes (if permitted by the organization) regularly. Copies of e-mails should only be sent to the relevant personnel. Restricting the use of the "copy to" facility means e-mail traffic is not increased unnecessarily, storage is not affected, and working time is not wasted by people who have to read e-mails to determine whether they are relevant.

- The types of file that may and may not be circulated via e-mail or instant messaging.

- Checking the correct e-mail address is selected to ensure it is being sent to the proper addressee.

The guidelines need to state how a breach can have fatal and expensive consequences to the IT system, for instance.

Reasons should be given for having the policy. This will help to establish the reasonableness of the policy. By demonstrating the potential legal liability, the employer is helping to reinforce the seriousness of any problems that might occur if an employee misuses the communication facilities. For instance, consideration might be given to ensuring employees are made aware that the policy is designed to make them more aware of the issues surrounding the use of the communications system, to explain why the policy has been formulated, and to explain the standards of behaviour from all employees when they use the communications system.

Relevant example: *Sangster* v *Lehman Brothers Limited* Case No 2201857/2002

The link to discipline

What should be included in the policy:

- The purpose of the disciplinary rules and procedure.

- To identify and set the boundaries to be expected of employees' behaviour at work.

- To ensure employees know what the consequences are if they breach the rules.

- To provide appropriate guidance for those employees or officers that are required to handle disciplinary matters.

The employer must set the limits, but is also required to ensure disciplinary issues are dealt with constructively, consistently and reasonably.

Employees must be made aware a set of rules exist and there is a link between their behaviour, what is expected of them and the disciplinary procedure. Other points to consider:

- Does the disciplinary procedure clearly state how the investigation will be conducted?

- Is the procedure fair, in accordance with natural justice, or is it open to being challenged?

- Any investigation undertaken by the organization before taking disciplinary action should be fair, appropriate and objective.

- The disciplinary procedure should be clear, have a set number of steps, and involve named posts (rather than named individuals) within the organization. Appeals should, preferably, be made to people with no knowledge of the initial decision. Transparency and fairness should be a hallmark of the procedure.

If you do not have a disciplinary procedure, the ACAS 'Code of Practice on Disciplinary and Grievance Procedures' will give some indication about where to start. The comments offered in this section are brief and do not include every issue that should be considered when devising a disciplinary procedure.

Relevant examples:

Dunn v *IBM United Kingdom Limited* Case No 230587/97

Reid, Rankin and Graham v *Compaq Computers Manufacturing Limited (now Hewlett Packard)* Case No S/103021/02, S/103022/02 and S/103023/02

Attachments

What should be included in the policy:

- Bandwidth can be taken up where employees send and receive large files attached to e-mail. For some organizations, such as marketing companies or similar departments within an organization, the transmission and receipt of such files will be a necessity. However, in many instances, the transmission of large files may be unnecessary and could be the cause of the temporary collapse of the infrastructure.

- Consideration should be given to advising employees about the restrictions relating to the limits imposed on the size of a mail box, and the effect such a limit may have on the sending and receipt of large files.

- Also, some types of file, because of the increased likelihood of containing viruses, may be banned. Examples include .exe or .pif files.

Receiving e-mail

What should be included in the policy:

- The policy will deal with a number of issues, many of which are included in this check list. Employees will be required to conduct themselves in such a way as not to breach any of the relevant prohibitions, such as disseminating discriminatory or sexual material, for instance. Consideration should be given to what action, if any, an employee should take if they receive an e-mail that is the subject of a prohibition.

- Where an e-mail is received that was not intended for the recipient, instructions should be given about what actions should be undertaken by the employee. For instance, it might be appropriate to delete the e-mail and inform the sender of the action.

- The policy should deal with how an employee deals with junk e-mail or "spam". Employees should be made aware that if they respond to the e-mail, it would confirm their address.

- Employees should be instructed how they must deal with incoming e-mail that contains inappropriate, offensive, obscene or pornographic material.

Frequency of checking and time away from the office

What should be included in the policy:

- Where an e-mail system is always on, then employees may well read and respond to e-mails as they enter their mail box. Where no such facility is provided, guidance should be given about how frequently e-mail should be read.

- E-mail is central to the way many organizations operate. As a result, consideration must be given to ensuring the job each employee performs is not suspended to the detriment of the organization when they are away for any reason, such as illness, attending courses or taking annual leave. Guidance should include:

  - Setting out the rules about who will read an employee's e-mail when they are not in the office. It is perfectly normal for postal mail to be read when somebody is not in the office, and e-mail is no different.

  - Employees should not feel a need to respond to e-mail immediately. Postal mail is rarely dealt with immediately it is received, and the content of most e-mails that are received does not merit a faster response time.

E-mail etiquette and protocol

What should be included in the policy:

- Advice as to how employees should draft the content of e-mails may be necessary. It might be useful to remind employees that, as with normal postal correspondence, the content of the e-mail should reflect clarity of thought, be written in clear English and be constructed professionally, which shall include checking the spelling and grammar. `

- Remind employees that although e-mail appears to be an informal mode of correspondence, nevertheless a slap-dash approach to the writing of an e-mail could have such serious consequences, that the organization may suffer a serious loss of reputation, and the individual employee may be in danger of being dismissed for their actions.

- Employees should be reminded that the accepted norms in relation to the use of e-mail should be observed, such as: the use of bold, capital letters or text written in red colour may be deemed inappropriate by the recipient. The use of such methods can be taken by some recipients to mean the sender is shouting. The aim is to ensure the content of the e-mail does not illustrate aggression or is so short as to appear to be unnecessarily abrupt.

Where the tone of a message may be inadvertently misunderstood, consideration should be given to communicating by telephone.

- Care must be given if e-mail is used to send personal messages (sending a redundancy notice by e-mail or text message has been used in the past, and the organization using this mode of communicating such a delicate message have damaged their reputation).

- Consider encouraging employees not to use e-mail to avoid talking to people, and ensure they are aware that using colours to emphasise points may well be lost at the recipients end, and the use of bold and italics may be more appropriate in such circumstances.

Personal use

What should be included in the policy:

- The employer must first determine whether to permit employees to transmit private communications by way of e-mail, instant messaging and for surfing the internet for private purposes.

- Whether permitted or not, the employer should make it clear that all communications, whatever the format they take, sent on the organization's system are the property of the organization.

- The employer must define what the organization deems to be private use and what is appropriate business use.

It is also appropriate to indicate prohibitions on use, such as:

- Not to give any information out about the organization or infer that a communication sent is an official document when it is clearly not the case.

- The employee is not to represent their personal opinions as those of the organization.

- Employees must not reveal or send any confidential or proprietary information.

- Not making any commitment that binds the organization.

The policy must set out what is and what is not acceptable, including (this list is indicative, not exhaustive):

- How to identify private e-mails.

- Limits on the size and type of files and material that can be downloaded from the internet or attached to e-mails.

- Downloading intellectual property from the internet, including software.

- What the employee may not do on the internet, such as prohibit the types of site that must not be visited (e.g. where a site contains hateful or objectionable material).

- Rules relating to looking at other employee's files and not altering the content of other employee's e-mails.

There are, it seems, three alternatives:

- Refuse to allow employees to use the system for e-mail, instant messaging and the internet for private use. If an organization decides to follow this option, a mechanism must be put in place to enforce the rule.

- Refuse to allow employees to use the system for e-mail, instant messaging and the internet for private use, but provide alternative computers for employees to use that are not part of the corporate network.

- Permit private use of the internet, e-mail and instant messaging over the corporate system, but complete privacy is not guaranteed to the employee. However, the employer can face problems with the conflicting requirements of legislation, including the *Human Rights Act 1998, Data Protection Act 1998, Freedom of Information Act 2000* and how to enforce what is considered "reasonable use". Care must be made to define how employees can use the communications system for private use.

Relevant examples

Morse v *Future Reality Limited* Case No 54571/95

Lois Franxhi v *Focus Management Consultants Limited* Case No 2102862/98

Escota v *Breil and Lucent Technologies* Electronic Business Law September 2003 Volume 5 Number 8 page 16

Monitoring

What should be included in the policy:

- Does the organization monitor any form of communications? If so, monitoring must be in accordance with the *Telecommunications (Lawful Business Practice)(Interception of Communications) Regulations 2000*.

- Employees must be made aware whether the organization monitors, how it monitors and for what purposes monitoring is undertaken.

- The reasons for monitoring must be made clear to employees. It is not possible to offer examples, because there will be a range of reasons that are unique to each organization. Suffice to say, the reasons for monitoring must relate to the criteria set out in the *Telecommunications (Lawful Business Practice)(Interception of Communications) Regulations 2000*.

Some examples include:

- The identification of inappropriate or excessive personal use that is contrary to the policy and to protect the organization's resources.

- Where an employee is absent from work.

- Checks made on the use of words that are defamatory or offensive.

- Additional scanning at the gateway of the address where the e-mail is destined.

Relevant examples

Miseroy v *Barclays Bank plc* Case No 1201894/2004

Confidentiality, trade secrets, industrial espionage

What should be included in the policy:

- Are employees made aware of the ease by which confidential and secret information can be sent electronically?

- Are employees aware of the principles of the *Data Protection Act 1998*?

- Have employees been made aware of the company guidelines for sharing and handling client information?

- Remind employees that if they send sensitive or confidential information, control of the information is lost once it is sent. If the information is so sensitive, consideration should be given to encrypting the files. However, such files cannot be checked for viruses, and the management of the relevant encryption keys must be considered carefully. If in doubt, send such sensitive information by courier, as in the past.

- Establish the categories of information that employees can transfer through the network communications system, including information from databases, personnel records or information received under a duty of professional confidence.

- Include rules in relation to the sending of confidential information received under a confidentiality agreement.

- Record all incoming and outgoing e-mails and instant messages in such a way that permits demonstration of authenticity.

- Sensitive material should be encrypted or sent by post.

- Adopt a digital signature facility if it is essential to prove authenticity of e-mail in certain circumstances. (If using digital signatures, particular care must be given to the control, storage and deletion of the private keys).

- When dismissing employees, ensure there is a procedure in place to prevent them from gaining access to their computer. If it is considered reasonable in the circumstances of the case, consider looking at the previous six months e-mail activities of any employee that leaves the company.

Relevant examples

Parr v *Derwentside District Council* Case no 2501507/98

Winder v *The Commissioners of Inland Revenue* Case No1101770/97/SM

Coleman v *Lansdowne Capital Limited & Alan Dargan* Case No 2201200/201 and 2204067/2001

Evidence and keeping records

What should be included in the policy:

- Documents in electronic format, including e-mails, can be "discovered" by outside parties to litigation. As a result, the organization should have a policy on the retention and disposal of documents.

- If there is such a policy, does it include electronic documents, e-mail documents and electronic attachments? If not, it should be considered a matter of importance to put a suitable policy in place quickly, and such a policy should refer to documents held in all formats, both hard copy and electronic files.

It is important to understand that the implementation and enforcement of the retention and disposal policy must be controlled at the highest levels within an organization. Individual employees should not be given the task of making decision as to which documents to retain or delete.

Organizations have a legal duty to retain and store certain types of document. Some organizations are also required to retain and store documents because of regulatory requirements. Ensure the same occurs with e-mail used in the business.

If it is impractical to store all e-mails electronically, print them off with full header information and get them signed by the member of staff dealing with the matter, although by doing this, other information, such as the meta data, will be lost. The point is, it is very easy to create printed e-mails that were never sent or received.

Ideally, the organization should take steps to ensure there is a complete and effective audit trail (for both e-mails, internet use and for all other documents created on the computer system).

Inappropriate use, time wasting, frolics and obscene material

What should be included in the policy:

- The policy should include instructions about downloading games, sending jokes, obtaining access to pornography, especially child pornography and using the organization's system to create, design and host a web site (including a web site that sells goods or services over the organization's infrastructure) – frolics of this nature can lead the organization into being joined as a third party to legal proceedings

- Apart from the wasted time and the use of computer storage such activities take up during the course of the day, it is possible to be put into an embarrassing position if criminal proceedings are considered by the authorities against an employee for downloading material that is obscene.

Is there a procedure for dealing with child pornography? If not, consider establishing a procedure. Issues to include (this list is not exhaustive):

- The immediate action that should be taken (there is a need not to contaminate any relevant evidence).

- Establish an officer with direct responsibility for dealing with such matters within the organization.

- Determine who is to be contacted internally and externally.

- Provisions for confidentiality amongst those that are privy to the incident.

Inappropriate use can include (this list does not include matters discussed elsewhere in this check list):

- Excessive use of e-mail and access to the internet for personal reasons, rather than work, such as undertaking personal financial transactions or commercial dealings.

- The regular transmission or receipt or both transmission and receipt of large files, such as photographs, video clips and other images.

- Professional misconduct.

Relevant examples

Atkins v *Director of Public Prosecutions; Director of Public Prosecutions* v *Atkins* [2000] 1 WLR 1427, QBD

Escota v *Breil and Lucent Technologies* Electronic Business Law September 2003 Volume 5 Number 8 page 16

Entering contracts unwittingly

What should be included in the policy:

- Do employees understand the basic elements of entering a contract? It is very easy to enter a contract in English law – an exchange of e-mails between two employees could be sufficient to bind each organization.

- Is there a policy in place allocating permission to officers and employees to enter contracts that will bind the organization? If so, limits will probably be set. Has the policy been extended to the use of e-mail, telephone and facsimile transmissions?

- If you do not want to provide suitable training, then you need to address this issue by establishing a method by which only certain employees have the authority to enter a contract.

There are some rules that you can educate employees to follow:

- Be clear by writing accurate, brief and unambiguous prose in plain English. Use simple language and write positively. Do not write using negatives.

- If you use vague language that is ambiguous, it might be construed to your disadvantage. Use short sentences to avoid being imprecise.

- The text should be logically set out so that both the sender and the recipient know who is responsible for doing what, at what time, how they are going to do it and who will pay.

Relevant examples

Hall v *Cognos Limited* Case No 1803325/97

Intellectual property rights

What should be included in the policy:

- Do employees understand they should not be abusing copyright? Are employees aware of what is and what is not protected by copyright? (Software; illustrations on web sites; in e-mails or in electronic files are just some examples).

- The organization should ensure all new content uploaded to its web site is checked for ownership of copyright. Inadvertently including the copyright content of another person or organization on the organizations web site may lead to legal action at worst, or an apology at best.

Copyright is infringed if complete files are downloaded from the internet and if e-mails incorporate copied text. The *Copyright, Designs and Patents Act 1988* provide for civil and criminal remedies when copyright has been infringed. Downloading files from the internet or copying text into an e-mail can breach copyright.

Relevant examples

Winder v *The Commissioners of Inland Revenue* Case No1101770/97/SM

Escota v *Breil and Lucent Technologies* Electronic Business Law September 2003 Volume 5 Number 8 page 16

Viruses

What should be included in the policy:

- Have employees been made aware of the risks with viruses? How well aware are employees of viruses and the damage that can be caused to the system?

- Does the organization permit the use of personal e-mail accounts, such as hotmail or instant messaging? If so, employees should be made aware of the risks that may arise from attachments that may contain viruses. Provisions should be made to provide information and a procedure to employees if they are permitted to receive e-mail from such accounts with attachments.

- The organization may usefully take the opportunity to explain what a virus is, together with the range of other destructive applications that could cause damage or loss of data.

Consider the risk of viruses with unauthorised software, both to your system and if you export the virus to others, which can make you liable in negligence for any damage caused. Also, consider designing a system to put e-mail attachments through a virus scanner before opening them.

On related matters, think about the system memory taken up, the lost time and cost of junk e-mail circulating within the company, such as jokes, animated cartoons, games and electronic postcards. Productive time is lost and, if sent to the outside world, may cause legal action to be taken. If employees download such material, they may introduce a virus.

Relevant examples

Gale v *Parknotts Limited* Case No 72487/95

Defamation

What should be included in the policy:

- The use of e-mail and instant messaging permit internal information to be sent to the outside world very easily. Employees must be made aware that e-mails in particular are not lost forever when they are deleted. As a result, there is a need to be careful about the content of e-mail messages.

- It is important to ensure that indecent, sexist or racist remarks are not made in the work place. Such remarks expose the organization to even greater threats if they are made in an e-mail.

Employee blogs

Increasing numbers of people are writing blogs, and employers cannot expect to prevent an employee from expressing their views. However, an employee can set out guidelines to employees. Consider:

- Setting out what is and what is not acceptable in a blog. For instance, employees should not discuss confidential information relating to the organization in their blog. An example would be an employee that informs readers of delicate negotiations between the organization and another entity that might cause the share price to rise or fall. It is important to ensure that an employee is made aware of the employer's right to take action against them if the employee makes comments that go beyond the guidance set out by the employer.

- Employees should be prohibited from mentioning whom they work for, whether they do it explicitly or implicitly. Employees should be made aware that they should not write about the organization, members of staff or its customers in terms that are not appropriate.

- The member of staff should clearly state that the blog represents their opinions only.

- Emphasis should be made on the need to ensure an employee does not write anything that brings the organization into disrepute. This should be linked to the disciplinary code.

Consideration should be given to ensuring the employees is aware of the relevant policies put in place by the employer, such as the equal opportunities policy, and how the relevant policies will affect the way the employer reacts if the employee publishes content on their blog that is contrary to the policy.

Relevant examples

Eggleton v *Asda Supermarket*

Exoteric Gas Solutions Limited and Andrew Duffield v *BG plc* [1999] LTL, The Independent, Thursday 24 June 1999

Western Provident Association Limited v *Norwich Union Healthcare Limited and Norwich Union Life Insurance Company Limited* Financial Times, 18 July 1997; The Times, 18 July 1997

Discrimination

What should be included in the policy:

- E-mail in particular permits people to circulate inappropriate comments that can demonstrate harassment of a sexual, racial, religious or sexual orientation nature, and provide evidence that an employer tolerates such attitudes in the workplace.

- There is no qualifying period for in such cases, and compensation is not subject to a maximum limit. Abusive e-mail can demonstrate sexual or racial harassment and provide evidence that an employer tolerates such attitudes in the workplace. Take steps that are reasonably practical to prevent employees carrying out such acts.

Relevant examples

G S Virdi v *The Commissioner of Police of the Metropolis* Case No2202774/98

Bower v *Schroder Securities Limited* Case No 3203104/99 and 3203104/99/S

Jayyosi v *Daimler Chrysler Limited* Case No 1201592/02

Training

In an ideal world, all employees and officers should be trained in these areas. Consideration should be given to providing refresher training every six or twelve months.

- Consider taking out insurance against liability for business disruption if defamatory material is inadvertently published.

- Ensure that employees know that their rights of access to computer systems must be given up on termination of employment or garden leave.

- Consider incorporating either confidentiality clauses or general disclaimers in company e-mails, depending on the nature of your business.

Relevant examples

Sangster v *Lehman Brothers Limited* Case No 2201857/2002

Carlucci v *Oracle Corporation UK Limited* Case No 2700870/03 and 2702150/03

Applying the policy

It is crucial to ensure the policy is applied equally against each employee. Failure to apply the policy uniformly may open an organization to legitimate attacks by employees in cases where, for instance, an employer deals with one set of employees (say women or workers) differently to another set of employees (men or managers). An emphasis must be on the equality of application of the policy.

Careful attention to following procedures is crucial.

Relevant examples

G S Virdi v *The Commissioner of Police of the Metropolis* Case No2202774/98

Sangster v *Lehman Brothers Limited* Case No 2201857/2002

Reid, Rankin and Graham v *Compaq Computers Manufacturing Limited (now Hewlett Packard)* Case No S/103021/02, S/103022/02 and S/103023/02

Corporate information to be included in external communications

All outgoing networked correspondence should include the following:

Company business letters

Section 349 (1)(a) of the *Companies Act 1985* states that every company will have its name mentioned in all business letters. Failure to include this information can make the company and the responsible individual liable to a fine, according to sub-sections 349(2) and (3). Section 351 requires the registration number and place of registration to be mentioned in all business letters. Failure to include this information can result in a fine for the company and the individual responsible according to subsection 351 (5). It is not certain whether Companies House has taken action against any company that has neglected to include this information in e-mails or on facsimile transmissions. However, it is prudent to include such information on e-mails to conform to the legal requirements.

Business Names Act 1985

Under the terms of this Act, a business must state the following information on all business letters, written orders for goods or services to be supplied to the business, invoices and receipts issued in the course of the business and written demands for payment of debts due in the course of business:

- Names of all the partners (if a partnership) (there are exceptions).

- Name of the individual trader if they trade under another trading name.

- An address for service in Great Britain for a document to be served on them.

Where an organization has a web site with all of this information already available on-line, it can be argued that a hyper-link to the relevant page on the web site might be sufficient to abide by these requirements.

Other information of relevant that should be included in communications include:

- Name and post of sender.

- Contact details, including telephone numbers (direct and via the operator).

- Facsimile number.

- E-mail address.

- Web address.

- Other relevant marketing materials.

The disclaimer

Organizations do not, in the normal course of events, add a disclaimer to correspondence sent by post, although the custom has developed by which disclaimers are added to facsimile transmissions, and now to e-mail correspondence.

A disclaimer seeks to distance the organization from the wrong or misguided actions of an employee. However, whether a disclaimer will succeed in achieving such an aim will depend on the particular circumstances of any given case. The reader is reminded that an employer is vicariously liable for the actions of its employees, and a great deal of case law has developed over the past 200 years in relation to this topic.

Arguably, a disclaimer can help to protect an organization if incorrect information has been sent out, for example. The format of a disclaimer will vary from one organization to another, depending on:

- The type of the risk, such as refusing to accept liability for defamatory comments (such a disclaimer is unlikely to succeed).

- Putting the recipient on notice that the sender has or has not got the authority to bind the organization contractually.

- The extent of the risk.

- The potential consequences that may follow.

A word of warning: once an e-mail leaves the system, the organization has lost the ability to control the content. This means the content can be changed by a number of people, and it is possible for the disclaimer to remain, together with the name and contact details of the originating organization. In the event of a dispute about the content of an e-mail, the disclaimer may not serve much purpose unless the originating organization can demonstrate the integrity of the content of the e-mail that was originally written and sent from their infrastructure. Thus particular attention should be paid to the system that can prove the integrity of the original e-mail that was created, because where there is a dispute about the content of an e-mail, the originating organization may have a very good defence if it can prove conclusively that the content of the e-mail in dispute was not sent by any of its employees.

It should be recalled that the content of a communication determines the type of documents it is. For instance, an e-mail can be:

- An internal memorandum.

- Official business by way of an external communication, and should be treated as official stationery, by being sent with the same corporate information that is contained on the stationery.

- A note to be added to a file.

- Private correspondence sent or received by employees.

It is not necessary to include a disclaimer on each of the examples cited above.

Security

Ideally, the security policy should be a separate document to the networked communications use policy. Having two documents helps to ensure employees do not conflate the requirements of the two policies, and (in an ideal world) should begin to treat security issues more seriously.

The range of issues to include in a security policy will be familiar to any IT security professional. Below is a list (it is not meant to be exhaustive) of some of the issues that should be included in the security policy:

- Clearly setting out who is responsible for what.

- Third party contractors and how they should be managed.

- Logging in and out of the system.

- The use and abuse of passwords; management of passwords.

- Protection of personal information in accordance with the *Data Protection Act 1998* and relevant Codes of Practice.

- Security when working from home or via a laptop.

- Personal equipment: the organization's policy on data entered on to equipment owned by an individual employee or contractor, bearing in mind the organization is liable as a data controller for the information stored on a computer owned by an employee.

- Equipment generally: provisions for insurance cover and policy dealing with precautions to prevent loss, misuse or theft.

- Portable equipment: provision of suitable security, such as password protection for the contents of laptops and such like if stolen, together with instructions on how to use when in public places.

- Monitoring activities.

- Out of hours policy.

- Backup of data and electronic files.

- Levels of security and classification of information.

- Procedure for members of staff leaving the organization.

- The need to secure confidential and secret data, both belonging to the organization and personal data of employees, customers and others held on databases (for marketing purposes, for instance).

Relevant examples

The failure of security is prevalent throughout all sectors, although the highest standards are usually set by such sectors as banking (although the banking sector has also suffered from poor security). As a result, there are far too many examples to cite in relation to security.

APPENDIX 2
EXAMPLES OF DISMISSAL

The following is a list of examples from the media where action has been taken by organizations. The reader will note that whilst there are examples from both the public and private sectors No organization is immune from this problem. This list is not exhaustive, but merely a sample.

The business world

September 2000, **Orange** dismissed 45 employees from call centres in Darlington and Peterborough and offices in Hertfordshire for allegedly distributing images of severed body parts to colleagues by way of e-mail.

November 2000, **Cable and Wireless** dismissed six employees and disciplined what is reported to have been "dozens of others" for sending offensive e-mails.

October 2000, **Merrill Lynch** dismissed 15 employees (eight men and seven women) for sending racist and pornographic material using the internal e-mail system.

January 2001, **Royal & Sun Alliance** dismissed ten employees and suspended 75 other employee in mid-December 2000 after an internal investigation found lewd e-mails circulating amongst members of staff, showing fictional TV character Bart Simpson in a sexual pose. Apparently a director of the company received a copy of the e-mail and the ensuing investigation led to the discovery of other such pictures, including one of the fictional cartoon characters Kermit the Frog and Fozzy Bear.

February 2001, **British Nuclear Fuels** is reported to have suspended three of its staff and six agency and contract workers for sending e-mails containing offensive material, thought to feature a character from the USA cartoon series *The Simpsons*. In December 2002, **British Nuclear Fuels** had cause to dismiss 11 employees who worked at the Sellarfield nuclear power station in relation to inappropriate use of the company e-mail system.

November 2001, it is thought that **Jaguar** dismissed 11 employees and disciplined a further 59 employees for circulating e-mails containing inappropriate content, and sent on to the parent company in the USA.

In October 2003, two workers at the **Courage** Fountain brewery in Fountainbridge, and an number of other employees at the Tadcaster plant in Yorkshire were dismissed after being caught distributing pornography by e-mail to other members of staff.

In April 2004, **Rolls Royce** dismissed three employees at its factory in East Kilbride, Scotland after they were caught downloading pornographic images from the internet.

In August 2004 it was reported that two unnamed employees of **Prudential**, working at the Stirling headquarters, were dismissed for allegedly dealing in drugs over the company's e-mail network. Apparently six further members of staff were either suspended or disciplined.

Law firms

In December 2000, Claire Swire, the girlfriend of assistant solicitor Bradley Chait in the firm of solicitors **Norton Rose** sent him, amongst other recipients, an e-mail containing a joke. The pair then exchanged a number of e-mails, which referred to a sex act she performed upon him. He sent a copy of the final e-mail to 12 colleagues, who in turn passed it on until millions read it. In this instance, the firm did not dismiss the employees concerned.

March 2001, four trainee lawyers, one in the Hong Kong office of **Herbert Smith** and three in the London office, circulated an e-mail that suggested a night cleaner has been murdered, then announced her replacement.

Patrick Smith is an Australian lawyer that was employed by the solicitors **Clifford Chance** in London. On 30 July 2003, Mr Smith was sent an invitation to attend a leaving party by his friend, Venn King, another Australian lawyer who worked for the solicitors Slaughter and May. He replied with the comment "Dude, [name of female] wants some of that double penetration action, so let me know when you and the old horse fat are around."" Mr Smith intended to send this reply to Mr King. However, he clicked the 'reply to all' icon, and the e-mail was sent to everyone on the list, who in turn forwarded it on to others. It is reported that those who received the e-mail understood that the person named by Mr Smith was a Japanese lawyer at another firm of solicitors, and that 'horse fat' means penis.

Public services

December 2002, the management of the **British Library** suspended nine members of staff from each of the sites it operates from (the main library in St Pancras, the newspaper library in Colindale and the document supply centre in Boston Spa, Yorkshire) for obtaining access to the internet to view pornography.

In September 2003, **Lothian Borders Police** investigated a number of employees when pornographic images were discovered on its computer system at its Edinburgh headquarters.

Civil service

Steve Webb, a spokesman for the Liberal Democrat party, obtained information covering 2002, showing the **Inland Revenue** investigated 211 cases of suspected misuse of computers and took action against 205 employees, and **Customs and Excise** investigated 101 cases and disciplined 42 employees. In most instances, the offences related to the misuse of e-mail.

In August 2004, it was reported that staff at the **Department of Work and Pensions** are alleged to have obtained access to two million pages of pornographic images in the previous year. 19 civil servants were dismissed and more than 200 were disciplined. One employee was said to have viewed 103,000 hardcore images. An investigation led to one criminal prosecution and a police investigation into two others.

In March 2005, two policemen (Mark Witcher, 30 and Andrew Lang, 31) from the **Surrey police force** were sent to prison for willful misconduct in public office, in that they had sex while on duty with a drunken woman. They had been called upon to help the woman, who drank 12 double Red Bull drinks. After the trial, Detective Chief Inspector Brian Russell subsequently told those attending a press conference that Andrew Lang had spent hours using a police computer to meet women through a dating site on the internet. He used the name 'Jedi Warrior' and sent sexually explicit e-mails.

Local government

In April 2001 a councillor from **Richmond-upon-Thames Council** was caught surfing for pornography using a laptop computer owned by the council. An internal investigation was set up by the borough's standards panel after a random check of staff laptop computers found the councillor had logged in to pornography web sites. The councillor was reprimanded for misusing council property. He was not identified.

In January 2003, **Flintshire County Council** began an inquiry into offensive images discovered on the Council's system. Apparently 47 members of staff were interviewed as part of the investigation.

In August 2003, Councillor Phil Grayson, who now represents **Wildridings & Central in Bracknell** as an independent, resigned from the Conservative party. Between March and May 2003, Mr Grayson exchanged a series of e-mails with a person called Julie Masters, who claimed to be a 23 year old woman looking for an e-mail friend who was an older man. When the correspondence ceased, the other person forwarded the e-mails to several councillors and the local newspaper. During the course of the exchange of e-mails, Mr Grayson included photographs of himself naked and wearing women's underwear.

APPENDIX 3
SOME USEFUL WEB SITES

Data protection

Information Commissioner	www.informationcommissioner.gov.uk
	www.dataprotection.gov.uk

Employment

Advisory Conciliation and Arbitration Service	www.acas.org.uk
Commission for Racial Equality	www.cre.gov.uk
Employment Appeal Tribunal	www.employmentappeals.gov.uk
Employment Tribunals	www.employmenttribunals.gov.uk
Employment Tribunals Service	www.ets.gov.uk
Equal Opportunities Commission	www.eoc.org.uk
European Industrial Relations Observatory	www.eiro.eurofound.ie
Incomes Data Services	www.incomesdata.co.uk
Institute of Employment Rights	www.ier.org.uk
International Labour Organization	www.ilo.org
Labour Relations Commission	www.lrc.ie
Trades Union Congress	www.tuc.org.uk
Whistleblowing	www.cfoi.org.uk/whistle.html

Electronic records management

Association for Information and Image Management	www.aiim.org.uk

List of useful web sites for electronic records

	www.nas.gov.uk/reckeep/PDFs/ ELECTRONIC%20RECORDS%20 bibliography.pdf
Public Record Office	www.pro.gov.uk
Records Management Society of Great Britain	www.rms-gb.org.uk
Society of Archivists	www.archives.org.uk

General

British Standards Institute	www.bsi.org.uk
Business Software Alliance, Inc. (trading in Europe as Business Software Alliance Europe)	www.bsa.org
BS 7799 Information Security Management (ISO/IEC 17799-2000)	www.c-cure.org
European Coalition Against Unsolicited Commercial E-mail	www.euro.cause.org/en
Institute of Chartered Secretaries and Administrators	www.icsa.org.uk
Mail Abuse Prevention System	www.mail-abuse.org

INDEX

Also of Interest from XPL

Data Protection Law – Second Edition

David Bainbridge BSc, LLB, PhD, CEng, MICE, MBCS, Reader in Law, University of Aston

Data Protection cases have developed the law in unexpected ways. David Bainbridge brings his classic text up to date with full reference to a huge range of materials. He brings his considerable experience as a writer and practitioner lecturer on these matters to produce a work that explains the context and implications of these important changes, whilst at the same time offering the substantive materials for further reference.

ISBN 1 85811 342 3   £48   New in 2005

Law for IT Professionals

Paul Brennan, Former General Counsel of the Federation Against Software Theft (FAST)

IT professionals should be concentrating on delivery IT. Now, however, professionals in every position or role are faced with a legion of complex legal issues from the internet to data protection, to copyright to EU Directives. They need something short to give them the bottom line. This book does that. The idea is to identify the key laws which are needed and describe them as briefly as possible (in a readable way), covering the essentials and highlighting the pitfalls to avoid.

ISBN 1 85811 322 9   £19.95   2003

Legal Protection of Software

Richard Morgan, Consultant, Cornwell Affiliates and Kit Burden, Partner, Barlow Lyde & Gilbert

By covering the life of a software product, the book provides all the individual or company would need. Like all the books Richard Morgan and Kit Burden have written, this title is legally authoritative and will be of great use to lawyers working in the area – especially commercial lawyers without expertise in IT. Full of checklists and flowcharts and other useful tools, it will prove invaluable to advisers and data users alike. Far more than just a law book, it will have a wide sale to business and their professional advisers.

ISBN 1 85811 294 X   £38

Intellectual Property and Information Technology Law

David Bainbridge BSc, LLB, PhD, CEng, MICE, MBCS, Reader in Law, University of Aston

Intellectual Property and Information Technology Law is a paper and electronic journal covering key developments in each of the major areas of Intellectual Property: *Trade Marks *Copyright *Patents *Designs *Licensing and *Computer Software. Essential developments in intellectual property law and procedure in the UK, Europe and worldwide are covered in an accessible and concise way. In-depth articles also cover issues of particular concern. Contact us for subscription details at the address below.

xpl publishing, 99 hatfield road, st albans, AL1 4EG

tel 0870 143 2569   fax 0845 456 6385   web: www.xplpublishing.com

Printed in the United Kingdom
by Lightning Source UK Ltd.
104698UKS00001B/103-159